So
TWILĬGHT

Song at
TWILIGHT

Vance Havner

Kingsley Press

Shoals, Indiana

Song at Twilight

Published by Kingsley Press
PO Box 973
Shoals, IN 47581
USA

Tel. (800) 971-7985
www.kingsleypress.com
E-mail: sales@kingsleypress.com

ISBN: 978-1-937428-96-9

Contents

Preface

A few years ago I wrote a batch of meditations published later under the title *It Is Toward Evening*. This new collection indicates that by now I am a little farther along on my journey and approaching twilight. Some of these reflections may sound more like sighs than songs; but, after all, "We that are in this tabernacle do groan" (1 Corinthians 5:4). But there is also a song, for "The night is far spent, the day is at hand" (Romans 13:12). The Christian is a pessimist as far as this world is concerned. He is not investing in a bank that will soon break! He is laying up treasure beyond the reach of moth and rust and thieves. This earth and its works will go up in flames, and we are not too excited about what will soon be one big cinder. We look for new heavens and a new earth, not the creation of science and politics and education and social reform, but straight from the hand of God. We sing, therefore, because what looks like twilight is but the prelude to eternal dawn.

VANCE HAVNER

CHAPTER 1

"Just a Song at Twilight"

RECENTLY in the home of a minister I listened to an old recording of favorite songs from the past: *In The Gloaming, Love's Old Sweet Song,* and others of tender memory. I went to a music store to buy that album but was told that it was no longer in production and could not be had. There were stacks of rock records, and all the demonic perversions of popular music were in abundance; but nowhere could I find the beautiful heart songs of a day when love lyrics were based on romance instead of sex. Evidently there was no demand from modern Sodom for *Just a Song at Twilight* or *Let Me Call You Sweetheart.*

Norman Rockwell's matchless artistry gave us for years on the covers of the *Saturday Evening Post* human interest masterpieces from American life. How he played on our heartstrings and stirred our recollections! But how many today care for these old-fashioned themes, and how few in this rat race can stop long enough to enjoy the paintings of Grandma Moses?

This is not mere nostalgia—sighing for a day that will never return. We could endure our loss if in its stead we had something better or even as good. But after listening to what goes for popular music now, we are persuaded that the worst of the Moonlight-and-Roses era is better than the best today.

It is evident that to be a famous singer these days and get rich at it you don't have to know how to sing. Just as farmers are paid for *not* farming, singers can make a fortune by *not* singing. What we are hearing now at the risk of our eardrums is neither heart nor art. Ernest Hemingway wrote about the Millennium of the Untalented and said that we are deluged with writers who can't write, actors who can't act, and singers who can't sing—and they're all making a million dollars a year! Auditoriums are packed to hear performers who know as much about music as a billy goat knows about Beethoven.

The distemper has invaded the churches in what goes for gospel music. It would be bad enough if jazz had remained in the night clubs amidst the darkness of heathenism transplanted from the African to the asphalt jungles. But when the church borrows both the language and the livery of Sodom, it is time to hang our heads in shame.

America has scant regard for the heritage of old songs, and the church begins to demean old hymns for their "irrelevance." *Rock of Ages* is a meaningless metaphor, we are told; and *There Is a Fountain Filled With Blood* is a relic of an outmoded theology. When both the nation and the church are too proud to sing the songs that warmed hearts for generations, it is no reflection on the old but it certainly shows up the new. If we must have relevance at the cost of reverence, we have made a poor bargain.

I am still trying to find *Just a Song at Twilight*. It is twilight with me and with this age. Just any song will not do for such a twilight.

CHAPTER 2

In the Land of Lanier

WHILE preaching in Brunswick, Georgia, I arose early on Sunday morning and made my way to "Lanier's Oak," the big tree where Sidney Lanier used to sit watching the marshes of Glynn. There he drew inspiration for much of his matchless poetry meditating before that vast expanse where "the marsh hen secretly builds in the watery sod."

I watched the sun rise and remembered Lanier's lines, "I will heartily lay me a-hold of the greatness of God." The Georgia poet wrote his lines back in the 1870s. I doubt that he could do as well now in the latter half of this century. A highway goes by the Lanier Oak, and even on Sunday morning trucks roar by blasting the calm serenity; and carloads of weekenders whirl by on their way to the beach. Who could think in such a bedlam, and who could be still long enough to contemplate the marshes of Glynn? The average motorist would give you a blank stare. "Sidney Lanier? Never heard of him." Ball players and television personalities they know but not this gentle soul who pondered the greatness of God. Sidney Lanier would be terrified if we set him down on that spot today. What would he think of zooming automobiles and screaming jets? But the marsh is still the marsh, and the marsh hen secretly builds there as of old. Over it all still broods an infinite calm, and we can still take hold of the greatness of God, for as Browning says:

> And I smiled to think God's greatness flowed
> around our incompleteness—
> Round our restlessness, his rest.

11

I stood one morning at Lanier's Oak and watched the tide come in. Slowly, gently, silently, every nook and cranny filled until the water almost reached the highway. I could not see whence it came, but I knew that not far away lay three thousand miles of the Atlantic Ocean. I thought of the line, "The lowest ebb is the turn of the tide." Today the church is at lowest ebb in many a day. I knew that beyond her dearth and drought lies the infinite ocean of God's grace. May the lowest ebb be the turn of the tide!

I once read of a ship stuck on a sandbar. It was a new boat with a new crew and they did not know much about seafaring. For hours they sweated and tugged and pushed and pulled, but the boat would not move. Finally they gave up. Next morning they found the vessel gently bobbing on the water. The tide had come in and had done gently, slowly, quietly, what all the striving of men could not do. Today the church, generally speaking, is stuck in the mud. All our feverish straining is to no avail. All sorts of schemes and projects for floating the craft come to nought. But there are laws of the tide and laws of spiritual renewal. Let the church go to prayer, repent, confess her sins, and call upon her God, and the ocean of his power will move in and set us afloat to carry the cargo of his grace and gospel to the ends of the earth.

Sidney Lanier wrote, "I will heartily lay me a-hold of the greatness of God." That reminds us of Isaiah's lament: "There is none ... that stirreth up himself to take hold of thee" (64:7). We are stirring up ourselves a-plenty with all sorts of religious rousements; but Isaiah would have us stir up ourselves with a purpose beyond ourselves, to take hold of God. So Paul bade Timothy not merely to stir up himself but to rekindle the flame of God within him.

Putting on a pep rally of the Sons and Daughters of I Will Arise is not the same thing as getting through to God.

CHAPTER 3

Springtime Journey

I did not want to leave North Carolina in mid-April with springtime bursting out everywhere in the tender beauty that is so long coming, lasts so briefly, and will not return for a year. I had a week or two to revel in the blossom-scented mornings and hear the robins celebrate the passing of winter and the coming of a better day. Then Sara and I took off on a preaching pilgrimage.

But we did not leave spring behind us. We rode through more of it, further advanced, through Georgia, Alabama, and Mississippi to New Orleans. No artist's brush or poet's pen has ever been able to portray the Old South in azalea and dogwood time. We have a new South about which I am not too enthusiastic, being an unconverted and unreconstructed old rebel; but magnolias and mockingbirds haven't changed, and antebellum mansions still hold their charm.

From New Orleans we rode through Louisiana rice fields and next day found us in the desolation of Southwest Texas, but even there spring brings a beauty of its own. A dear friend met us in El Paso and brought us to Hobbs, New Mexico, where I preached for a week. Every morning I took a walk through a lovely residential area. The trees were different in a dozen shades of green and the flowers were exquisite. Everything is planted, but man has made the desert to blossom as the rose. There were picture postcard sunsets and the crisp nights made welcome the warm, clear days.

Again we were transported by our friend to Raton where another good brother met us and took us to Colorado Springs. Nearly five hundred miles of open spaces altogether were tinted with spring's new green. Not much was stirring except the tumbleweeds that rolled across the highway. You'd think that here is room enough for the population explosion if enough water could be found!

I preached for a week in Colorado Springs and stayed in a room facing Pike's Peak in its snowcapped splendor. I discovered a dirt road away from traffic and travel where each morning I strolled early in full view of towering majestic peaks. Wild rabbits with enormous ears scampered and roadrunners flew awkwardly everywhere. I love the song of the Western meadowlark, quite different from the "flying shaft of sound" with which John Burroughs used to say the Eastern meadowlark greets the spring.

Time came to move again and we boarded the *Denver Zephyr*, one of the last good trains, with its dome car giving us a wide view of Nebraska and Iowa, their rich farm lands waking to the new season. A wet, dismal day in Chicago and then off again to Washington. The rugged mountains of West Virginia came first next morning, and finally we rolled into the capital just a little past cherry-blossom time. From there we took a bus through Virginia and closed the circuit into the South again across those miles where valiant men fought and died a century ago, and one still wonders who was right.

I could hardly wait next morning at home to return to my bird-watching. I was just in time. I stood under a tree while overhead in full view my first wood thrush of the new year gave one of the best concerts I have ever heard. Not far away a scarlet tanager warbled gently, and nearer still Parula and black-throated blue warblers did their *zee, zee, zee-eep* and *zur, zur, zee*. Later I heard an ovenbird, and then a black-throated green warbler invited me with his *ah, see, listen to me*.

To cap the climax, I returned to dear Charleston for the weekend to bask in memories of thirty years ago. Next morning I watched an unforgettable sunrise over the water down by the Battery. Charleston was in the midst of racial strife with a curfew on each night. I thought of all the misery of this unhappy world and recalled the song, *The World Is Waiting for the Sunrise*. Indeed, the world is waiting, whether most men know it or not, for "sunrise tomorrow"—both Son-rise and Sun-rise—when the Sun of Righteousness shall arise with healing in his wings (see Malachi 4:2.)

Even so, come, Lord Jesus.

CHAPTER 4

Katydids

ALTHOUGH I live in the middle of town, I go to bed each night in these last August days of a waning summer to the music of katydids outside my window. I doze off to sleep to the incessant affirmation that *Katy did* and *Katy didn't*. It seems so out of place here in this bustling city. Sometimes I slip into dreamland as my mind goes into a fifty-year reverse and I'm a boy again growing up out in the country. I've had my supper of cornbread and milk and I can barely make it to bed, I'm so deliciously sleepy. There wasn't a sedative or a tranquilizer in the house! We went to bed at a decent hour and went to sleep unaided. Nobody understands sleep to this day, but what a wonderful arrangement of the Almighty when he granted us this boon! As with all the other great simplicities, no satisfactory substitute has ever been found.

So the katydid lulled me to slumber 'way back in the dear days beyond recall. Maybe it was the week of the revival meeting at old Corinth Church. The night had been hot, the sermon long, and the hour was late. We drove home in the old surrey and this weary lad thought we'd never get there. I hardly knew when we arrived but somehow got my clothes off and into bed in a stupor. There were some years long after when I would have given everything for a few hours of the sleep I once took for granted!

This old world has turned over many times since this country boy went to sleep listening to *Katy did* and *Katy didn't*. In the delirium of these weird days the simple sounds that still survive the holocaust of Progress are welcome as never before. In this madhouse of computers, jets, atom bombs, riots, rock-and-roll, anarchy, drug addicts, the new morality, rotten politics, and defunct theology, the sound of a katydid is a gentle reminder that some things haven't changed. And what hasn't changed is far more important than what has!

The katydid, like the wood thrush I heard early this morning, belongs to the elemental things like sun and air and water. For all our inventive wonders we have devised nothing better. My Lord, when he preached in Galilee, talked of flowers and birds and bread and salt and light. He would do the same today, for we need them all as much as ever; and nothing can take their place. Most of us know that—except a few pompous poor souls educated beyond their intelligence who fancy they have outgrown these homely things just because we have split the atom and have gone to the moon. It might help some of these sophisticates and reduce them to their right size if they had to lie for an hour or so each night and listen to the katydid. If they are not beyond redemption point, their fevered souls might still be reached and calmed with the peace that passes understanding.

The psalmist surveying the heavens in reverent awe has been replaced by the space expert planning the next excursion into the skies. Now an astronaut may be able to worship with the Eighth Psalm on his lips; but if we have to give up either the psalmist or the astronaut, we'd be better off with David on the Bethlehem hills than with the spacemen at Cape Kennedy. We shall be in a sad plight if we gain a world of astrophysics and lose our souls somewhere among the constellations.

Even the song of a katydid on a summer night can go a long way toward restoring our perspective and rearranging our scale of values if we are not too nervous and restless to be still and listen.

Chapter 5

Extra Pennies

TODAY I lingered before the candy counter trying to make up my mind. I do not eat much candy, and there was such a bewildering array of sweets that I had difficulty deciding which tidbit I wanted. When I was a boy, there was not much to choose from! Yet there were problems even then. Mother used to send me to the tiny store up the road with a few eggs. She told me that if there were any pennies left over after my purchases I might spend them for candy. Away I went hoping the price of eggs was up and the price of groceries down. If there were pennies left over I deliberated long as to which of the few sticks of candy I might choose from the little showcase. There never was enough money or candy for I didn't have just a sweet tooth, I had a set of sweet teeth both uppers and lowers!

Somebody ought to preach a sermon on leftovers. He could talk about the "handfuls of purpose" that Boaz left in the field for Ruth (2:16); or the twelve baskets full of food that remained after Jesus fed the multitude. Some leftovers are not popular; and one might relate the story of the minister who always returned thanks when leftovers were served by saying, "Lord, we thank thee for thy continued blessings."

But I am thinking of pennies left over. So much money will buy so many groceries. That is a hard fact. But if the price of eggs exceeds the cost of the groceries, ah, what a good fortune that was to a country boy! It is the margin above and beyond the grim realities of life that gives it zest and tang and makes all the rest endurable. For me as a boy, a hot walk up a dusty country road found ample compensation in a couple of sticks of candy; and life's drudgery is not without its attendant delights. One could never add up the innumerable little things—a kind word here, a loving thought there, the caress of a loved one, watching a sunset, a bird song in springtime, a precious Bible verse aglow with new meaning, an answered prayer—who could ever enumerate life's extra pennies, the surplus not on the regular schedule, the bonus after we have already collected our pay!

A spoiled generation that has had everything has no appreciation for what I am writing here, just as today's children are surfeited with candy and everything else. It did not take much to make us kids happy years ago, and today nothing makes most people happy. Some mods today would sneer at the candy, loot the store, and then burn it down!

But a happy heart like a country boy had lies in the simple enjoyment of God's daily blessings and the extra delights when there are pennies left over. Our God is not a taskmaster. He is our Father, and he does not keep his children by a cold, hard set of rules and ledgers. He has not computerized the business. All my life he has run up the price of eggs and lowered the prices of groceries and left extra pennies ever since I trudged that old country road when like James Whitcomb Riley I was

so happy and so pore.

CHAPTER 6

The Tests of the True

AT lunch in a restaurant today I saw a pot of flowers so exquisitely textured and skilfully colored that only by closest examination could I discern that they were artificial. Throughout my meal I pondered how in this synthetic age we have developed the art of simulation to a degree that deceives even the experts. The old motto has been reversed and now the slogan of the times is "To seem rather than to be."

Satan is the master deceiver, the mock angel disguised as an angel of light. He does not plow up the wheat in our Lord's parable; he plants tares that resemble wheat so closely that few know the difference, and the final separation is left to angels. When Moses performs miracles, Jannes and Jambres are on hand to match the performance (see 2 Timothy 3:8). Our Savior repeatedly warned against deceivers in the last days.

But what struck me most as I surveyed these false blossoms was the disturbing reflection that they were even more attractive than many real flowers I see. They were cleaner, fresher, more uniform and symmetrical than some roses fresh from the garden. The reason is obvious. They are protected from wind and weather, never exposed to dirt and bugs and blowing wind or rain. Shielded from the elements, they run no risk of being withered or soiled. The false may be prettier than the true.

In the spiritual world this comparison exists. We have imitation Christians, phony disciples who go through all the motions of the good life, recite all the creeds, sing all the songs, pray all the prayers. And just as a mortician can make a dead man look better than a living man, so these artificial saints may appear more godly than the true. They have never been exposed to real

warfare in the heavenlies, conflict with the powers of darkness. Sometimes Christians are so battered in the storms of evil that they appear less attractive than these plastic saints. They are often defeated and torn by temptation. Simon Peter was not as "pretty" as some sheltered Pharisee in the temple spotless in his robes and phylactery. But let these synthetic flowers be exposed for a day to all that besets a rose in the garden and what a bedraggled sight evening would reveal!

Our Lord spoke of those who make a fair profession but have no root or depth and give way in the day of temptation and persecution.

There are also genuine flowers that grow in hothouses protected from the storms. We have hothouse Christians who have never endured hardness as good soldiers of Jesus Christ. They may win prizes in exhibitions, and they may look better than some windblown varieties outdoors; but the storm shows them up if ever they face it.

Something else will show up both the hothouse and the artificial saints. There is coming a time when "the day shall declare it" (1 Corinthians 3:13), and every man's life will be tested of what sort it is. There will be a lesser reward for the hothouse saint who played it safe. And for the manufactured sort who often put up a far better appearance, who even prophesied, cast out demons, and did many wonderful works, there will be the fearful word of him who is never deceived, "Depart, I never knew you."

… in time of temptation … (Luke 8:13).

… in that day … (Matthew 7:22).

These are the Tests of the True.

CHAPTER 7

Walling Up the Fireplace

T HE little old house where I grew up still stands. The front room had a fireplace; and there we gathered of an evening, Dad and Mother, my sister and brother, and I. The cat sat with us, and Father used to enjoy talking to the feline member of the family as though everything he said were understood. We had evening devotions there. Sometimes a neighbor dropped in. We had neighbors then. Today we live in apartments and hardly know who is next door. We have never been closer together—and farther apart!

When radio came only I remained at home with Dad and Mother. We enjoyed that old set with its three tuning knobs and big amplifier. *Amos and Andy* and *Fibber McGee and Molly* were favorites. Father never sat up late, for he stuck doggedly to his early-to-bed, early-to-rise routine. He was not too healthy, never became wealthy—but he was wise.

Eventually Father left us one winter for his heavenly home, and soon my brother and his family moved in. The old fireplace was walled up and a heater put in its place. There were some good reasons for that. Before the fireplace you froze on one side and fried on the other. The heater warmed things up more evenly. Now I'm in an apartment where a flick of a switch soon makes everything cozy.

But I miss the old fireplace. Nobody ever had an inspiring thought staring at a heater. Warm air blowing through a vent is not conducive to reflection. There was something about watching dying embers while shadows danced on the wall. There was no distracting television, and families got to know each other before the fire. Our eardrums were spared blasts of jazz and raucous

23

commercials. (Why must they split our ears as though everybody were nearly deaf?) We didn't have to talk. There was something about the fire that welded us together in a fellowship that needed no words to cement it.

I am glad that some newer homes are putting in fireplaces. It could be a faint indication that some mortals are regaining their sanity. But generally we have walled up the fireplace today in more ways than one. We are closing our doors to reflection, meditation, quiet communion, and we are paying a dear price. Newer devices have brought more comfort and ease, but our nervous spirits turn in all directions for peace and serenity. Experts and diplomats meet to discuss our problems but get nowhere. Maybe they should put a fireplace in the conference room! Our homes are breaking up and the generation gap widens. Maybe we had better install fireplaces in the living room and rule out TV long enough to get acquainted! We wouldn't miss much anyway! Preachers would do well to muse while the fire burns until the holy bone-fire that Jeremiah felt ignites within them. Television has taken a toll even among the clergy, and a fireplace would be a blessed exchange for the late, late show.

Innumerable ills have befallen us since we walled up the fireplace. I think I'd like to return to the old front room back home, remove the heater, and start a blaze. I'd like to sit in the old rocker and watch the glowing embers. It might take awhile to recapture what I have lost in these years, but it would go far in restoring my soul.

It's time to reopen the fireplace!

5/23/2023

8:46pm

CHAPTER 8

A Candle in the Night

A thunderstorm knocked out the electric power and our apartment was in the dark. We lit the candle which we keep for such emergencies. Electric power is quite a wonderful thing these days, but all our gadgets fail when a transformer burns out. Off goes the air conditioning, the refrigerator, the clock, the television set. What slaves we are to all our gimmicks and how dependent on electricity! A candle looks feeble against the darkness, but it has one asset: it burns on its own power and is not beholden to the vast system that can be immobilized by one thunderstorm.

My little candle set me thinking. Sir Edward Grey said at the beginning of World War I, "The lamps are going out all over Europe." They are going out all over the world today. Our vast systems are failing, and the gigantic political setups are crumbling before the storms of anarchy. Man's power machines are giving way and humanity gropes in darkness. Sad is the plight of any man who has no candle that can make its own light and is not dependent on the system.

The psalmist wrote, "Thou wilt light my candle: the Lord my God will enlighten my darkness" (Psalms 18:28). Of course, they probably had no candles in Bible times—only the crude lamps of antiquity—but the principle is the same. Blessed is the man who is not dependent these days upon the light of this world. The power system of this age is imposing enough with its culture, its science, its politics, its technology, its sophistication. The whole business is cracking up in the tempest of these times. But there is a candle that draws its light from another source. God's Word is a lamp unto our feet and a light unto our path. Jesus Christ is the Light of the world, and if he lives within us we are not slaves to this world's system for our illumination. A candle may seem a frail thing, and there are those who ridicule the Christian's faith, so enslaved are they to the power structures of this age. But all hell cannot put out the Christian's candle. Many a man, sick and disillusioned with all this world has to offer, has turned back to the simple faith of his mother and has found a light that stands him in good stead when the hurricanes of life knock out man's elaborate transformers.

It is a good thing to have a candle in the dark. And never has darkness settled as black as it is today. Just when man thought he had perfected his power system, the typhoon struck. Adversity, trouble, sickness, sorrow—all these can knock out our human comfort—but the soul that on Jesus hath leaned for repose is not left alone in the night. He has a candle when the lights go out.

Somebody went to a coal mine to look for a friend. They told him, "He is a Christian, and you'll find him down there in the dark somewhere but likely he'll be singing." Down, down, down he went and thought as he went, "If he's singing in these dungeons his song must be 'Down in a gulf of dark distress we wretched sinners lay.'" But finally he heard singing. He caught the words of an old gospel song:

> Here shines undimmed one blissful day
> And all my night has passed away.

That Christian miner had his candle with him!
Blessed is the man whose inner light is generated from another source unaffected by the thunderstorms of these tragic times.
It is a good thing to have a candle in the night.

5/24/2023
2:57 Am
Wed.

CHAPTER 9

Scraping an Apple

D ID you ever "scrape" an apple? There filters back to me through the years beyond recall a memory of my grandmother. She liked to cut an apple in two and scrape out the inside a spoonful at a time. The apple half formed a bowl, and the operation made tedious peeling unnecessary. Grandmother enjoyed eating apples that way, and as a little boy it fascinated me.

In all the years since, I have never seen anybody scrape an apple. This harried and hurried generation of nervous wrecks munches the apple, peeling and all. Who has time to leisurely scrape it! That went out long ago with whittling and the parlor lamp. Not long ago I revived the art, and for awhile I kept the doctor away every day with a scraped apple. It is a delicate operation, and I am sure it could be perfected into a dainty art with a sharp knife and dexterity skillful enough to get out all the meat and leave only a paper-thin shell.

Scraping an apple is symbolic of something far greater—the calm and unhurried enjoyment of life's simpler pleasures. What it symbolizes is as out-of-date as the symbol. Nobody has time for the common satisfactions, and who is calm or unhurried? This is not the lament of old age, for my first book, *By the Still Waters,* written thirty-five years ago, sounded the same note. I have always sought to make a place for the song of a bird, the beauty of a sunset, the peace of solitude, the benediction of a stroll along a country road. As the insane tempo of this maniacal age speeds to a demonic delirium tremens, it becomes next to impossible to find time or place even to scrape an apple!

Recently I received a card from an old friend, a former deacon in my church long ago. He is now eighty. He had heard a radio sermon of mine and he wrote something to this effect:

> It sounded so old-fashioned, it reminded me of days long ago
> on the farm. It was a hot day and I had been breaking up new
> ground. I found a watermelon, not the present-day pampered,
> petted, protected, sprayed and disinfected kind—just a water-
> melon. I had no knife so I busted it open on a rock and how
> refreshing it was on a scorching summer day!

Well, eating an old-fashioned watermelon back on the farm
belongs in the same category as scraping an apple. All this is part
of another age, and this generation would read all this with a
blank uncomprehending stare. I can only pity them, for they were
born too late. It has been a long time since I have seen anybody I
could scrape an apple with. The *in* crowd and the jet set dismiss
such corny remnants of an outmoded age as still around waiting
to die. One could use a few apple scrapers and whittlers with
their calm counsel and seasoned wisdom, for this age of progress
has mired in the mud on its way to a vaunted millennium.

And now I think I'll scrape an apple.

CHAPTER 10

Mourner

I am staying this week in a Southern town where once there was a lovely park with a lake and ducks, bridges and benches and singing birds. I used to browse there and so I set out in anticipation to revisit that restful spot. But no more. The demon of progress has invaded those peaceful domains. As I feared, another highway had to be built to accommodate the hordes of motorists, and it has split the park in two. What remains on both sides is a morass of weeds, broken walks, and pollution. Each morning I stand amid the ruins, a mourner at the bier of another casualty in the wholesale slaughter of our spots of beauty.

This is no isolated case. In my hometown I used to roam acres of deep woods with a pond and a deserted old mill in the center of it. Readers of my earlier books will recall many meditations written in that retreat. They will also remember The Boy, that little nephew who was my constant companion on those happy jaunts. Well, The Boy is now a man with a daughter of his own, and the old mill was destroyed and the woods torn up by an army of bulldozers like the invading Huns of old. Now there is a complex of highways with mad motorists insanely pursuing each other; and for most of them it makes no difference, for they wouldn't see the trees or hear the birds if the woods were still intact. Sometimes I walk out that way to mourn at that bier and lament the passing of something very precious to me. Of course the chamber of commerce and the highway department would only stare at me in uncomprehending amazement if I expressed my grief to them. I would seem as one "tetched" in the upper story—a hopeless throwback in the path of progress.

There is another spot in New Jersey where, ten years ago, I

reveled one week in springtime in woods full of warblers. It was just across the road from the motel where I stayed, and I could hardly wait of a morning to get lost in that idyllic hideout. Last year I visited it again only to find another swamp foul and defiled and forsaken. For old times sake I went back each morning to mourn at that bier and recover what little I could from the disaster.

This morning I stood in the wreckage of the park I used to enjoy. There was a lonely catbird, and the chipmunks squeaked and darted to cover, startled that any intruder should trespass on their territory. The lake has grown up in weeds and what water remains is filthy. All three of these deserted beauty spots are illustrations of a tragedy—the fading away of the quiet place of meditation before the juggernaut of the new age. Something has gone that will not return in this dispensation, and we can only mourn at its bier.

There is now a last-minute effort to try to salvage something from the shambles of pollution. *Ecology* has become a familiar word, and politicians will squander billions to purify air and water. We are probably too far gone, and it is doubtful whether this poor generation has what it takes or cares enough to recover our lost beauty. Millions who pollute their bodies with tobacco, liquor, and drugs will hardly care enough to cleanse their environment. Our worst pollution is not outer but inner, and any people as rotten on the inside as we have become will not likely bother much about swamps and sewerage.

But while I mourn at a bier I rejoice, for it will not always be like this. My Lord will return to reign on this earth. The program will not be in the hands of experts then, thank God, and there will be a new environment. The Bible portrays a redeemed earth, cleansed of defilement, rid of violence among beasts and men, free of disease and death with all evil under control. We should do whatever we can to clean up things now, but my soul awaits a better day—the restitution of all things, at the manifestation of the sons of God. All creation stands on tiptoe awaiting that day. Even so, come, Lord Jesus!

CHAPTER 11

Three Men Who Started Something

IT was a wise old monk who asked Martin Luther, "Dost thou believe in the forgiveness of sins?" When Luther replied that he did, von Staupitz exclaimed, "Ah, but you must not only believe in the forgiveness of David's sins and Peter's sins, for this even the devils believe. It is God's command that we believe our own sins are forgiven us!"

"From that moment," says D'Aubigné, "light sprung up in the heart of the young monk at Erfurt."

"I believed," said Luther, "that my sins—even mine—were forgiven me."

Two hundred years later a plain Moravian pastor, Peter Bohler, asked the troubled John Wesley, "Do you know Jesus Christ?"

"I know," replied Wesley, "that He is the Savior of the world."

"True," answered the Moravian, "but do you know that he has saved *you?*" Wesley said he did but confessed in his *Journal* that he feared they were empty words. Later, at Aldersgate, he came to the assurance "that he had taken away my sins, even mine!" In the power of that witness, and on the strength of that assurance, he transformed England.

One hundred years later a lad under old-fashioned conviction of sin started to church on a Sunday morning. A snowstorm prevented him from reaching the church he had meant to attend and he slipped into a little Primitive Methodist chapel. There were only a few present, and the regular pastor failed to arrive. A very plain substitute ("a shoemaker or something of that sort") talked for a few minutes about looking unto Jesus, ran out of something to say, and in desperation shouted to the lonely lad under the gallery, "Young man, you're in trouble! Look to Jesus Christ! Look! Look! Look!" Charles Haddon Spurgeon looked and was saved.

The monk, the Moravian, the makeshift, here is a sort of apostolic succession. Here are certain tremendous lessons for all of us. The importance, for one thing, of sticking to the point. If these men had wandered, had dodged the issue, had hesitated lest they offend the needy soul before them, three of the mightiest giants who ever strode across the pages of church history might have missed their way. Are we as insistent nowadays that hungry hearts know for themselves that their sins are forgiven? In our haste to add more church members we fail so often to do a thorough job of getting sinners through to assurance of salvation and the witness of the Spirit. What a flock of would-be Luthers and Wesleys and Spurgeons we ordain into the ministry before they have ever had an encounter with Jesus Christ! We persuade young volunteers to say with Isaiah, "Here am I; send me" (Isaiah 6:8), before they have ever cried, "Woe is me!" (6:5).

These three men never dreamed of the repercussions that would follow their counsel on these three occasions. They had no idea that the pebbles they dropped upon those waters would send undulations to earth's farthest shores. You never know what potential lies locked in the breast of that wriggling youngster in your Sunday school class. But even the humblest soul, whether ever heard from or not in the years to come, is worth your best effort.

And how this should rebuke us for thinking a handful of listeners is not worth our best! The attendance at Aldersgate and Artillery Street would give a modern promotion expert nervous prostration. A preacher who is too big for a little crowd would be too little for a big crowd!

Speaking of chain reaction, it is noteworthy that somebody was reading Luther's *Commentary on Romans* in that Aldersgate meeting when Wesley saw the light.

That monk who faced Luther with the real issue could still hear the echoes if he were here today!

CHAPTER 12

Musings of a Migrant

STROLLING down the street in a little Southern town I came to a picture in a show window. Whatever its rating among the art critics might be I do not know, but I do know that it spoke to my heart and I have not forgotten it. It was a painting of an autumn scene on a northern lake, aflame in red and brown and gold. Rising from the tranquil waters were several wild ducks starting on their long journey south. The first touch of winter had come, and these wise creatures got the message. They read the signs and lost no time taking off for a warmer clime.

It brought to mind the immortal lines of Bryant to a waterfowl:

> He who from zone to zone
> Guides through the boundless sky thy certain flight
> In the long way that I must tread alone
> Will lead my steps aright.

It brought also to the mind of this preacher that he is a migrant in this old world and that the time draws nearer for his departure. I am a pilgrim and a stranger, an exile and an alien, and I have no home down here—"no certain dwelling-place" (1 Corinthians 4:11).

We Christians forget so easily that we are not citizens of earth en route to heaven but citizens of heaven temporarily residing on earth. The wild duck is not too attached to a northern lake; he knows that he will be leaving at summer's end. God's people sit loose to this world, for they are leaving at the close of the season. No wonder Paul writes:

33

"But this I say, brethren, the time is short: it remaineth, that both they that have wives be as though they had none; and they that weep, as though they wept not; and they that rejoice, as though they rejoiced not; and they that buy, as though they possessed not; and they that use this world, as not abusing it: for the fashion of this world passeth away" (1 Corinthians 7:29).

To one past his threescore and ten the picture in the show window holds a poignant charm. For all its "dangers, toils and snares" I have enjoyed my stay in this old world. Spoiled by sin and soiled by sinners it is but a wreck of its earlier beauty—but it still holds much that reminds us of its former glory and of the grandeur yet to come when it shall be redeemed. The wild ducks leave the northern lakes, but they expect to return. I am anticipating my migration to a better realm, but I plan to come back to reign with the saints on a restored earth. Then one day there will be new heavens and a new earth, and that will be our eternal home. What a prospect! No wonder the heart beats faster in the autumn of our days when so much lies ahead!

These falling leaves, the flaming sumac, this nip of winter in the air—all these suggest to the Christian what this world knows nothing of. It is the tragedy of the church that we have lost our pilgrim character and driven down our tent pegs in these poor lowlands as though we were here to stay. If we understood what transients we really are it would put everything in a new perspective and add a zest to our present stay that so few Christians know.

Cheer up, my fellow migrants, it will soon be time to move!

5/24/23
3:46AM
Wed
HB
Friday

CHAPTER 13

A Better Cup of Tea

SOME time ago a preacher friend of mine gave me a recipe for a better cup of tea. He told me how to mix certain ingredients I had never tried before and the results were revolutionary. Sara and I have been drinking the new tea ever since, and like it better all the time. I have been telling people about, it and everybody who has tried it is enthusiastic. This week I recommended it to the pastor of the church where I am preaching and to the song leader. Both became ardent "converts." So the word gets around, and a new club of tea drinkers forms by passing on the word from one to another. There is no advertising campaign—it is just that we have found a good thing and we share it.

Here is a simple illustration of how the gospel is spread. Somebody becomes a Christian and finds every need met in Christ. He begins to tell others what he has found. They try it and tell still others. The word gets around. There is no need to fear failure, for no man has ever been disappointed in Jesus Christ. The early church grew by this simple method. Modern advertising and public endorsement over the news media may sell a product, but nothing beats personal testimony. Satisfied customers are the best salesmen. Just so, the church may loudly and widely publicize the gospel, and indeed we should; but along with that must be the witness of Christians who speak from first-hand experience. There is great danger that we may depend on big-scale promotion of Christianity and neglect the best method ever known—the system Andrew used on his brother Peter, and Philip on Nathanael.

After my experience with a better cup of tea I found myself asking, "Why is it so easy to recommend a better cup of tea

35

and so difficult to tell others what Christ means to us?" I know there is the ingrained reticence to talk about spiritual matters; but surely the greatest discovery a man can make should not be hidden, shut up in his own heart with a lock on his lips! If only Christians shared that experience like they share other good things that happen to them it would do what all the promotion projects and programs can never do.

The tragedy is that so much Christianity today is only a mental acceptance of the gospel—a performance but not an experience. It is an impersonal head belief but not a warm, glowing fellowship with the living Christ. Such Christianity does not make flaming witnesses eager to pass on the joy of their new life. Missions are an abstraction, but a live missionary translates it in flesh and blood. Evangelism is a cold subject unless it is embodied in an evangelist. The Word became flesh and dwelt among us and must be embodied in living people to reach others. A printed recipe on how to make a better cup of tea may get some results, but a live enthusiast who puts on a demonstration is the best salesman. It is better to have your cup of tea on hand and invite your friends to try it.

If only we had more convinced Christians who have tasted and found that the Lord is good—that Christ is their life, their bread, their meat, their drink—and who tell what they have found wherever they go! It sells a better cup of tea to have tried it and found it good—and then to recommend it to everybody. Nothing spreads the gospel like a Philip finding Nathanael and reporting, "We have found him" (John 1:45).

There are professional teatasters, I am told, but we do not need their counterpart in Christian experience. We are not meant to sip lightly of this truth and that but to drink regularly and habitually of the Living Water.

We have a treasure in earthen vessels and something to pass on worth infinitely more than a better cup of tea!

*Vance should have
Shared the
recipe*

*5/28/23
Brian
Frew*

CHAPTER 14

The Meditating Bird

SARA and I spent a week at Corpus Christi, Texas, in early autumn. Our motel room looked out on the lovely bay where water birds were in abundance. I am not well posted on that branch of the bird world since my specialty has been songbirds, but gulls and plovers and sandpipers and all the host of feathered beachcombers can be very fascinating.

Early in the week we were attracted by a lonely crane of some sort who stood motionless by the hour looking out on the water. He never moved a muscle and appeared wrapped in solitary contemplation. I am sure he was looking mainly for something to eat, but I fancied him to be in deep thought. We began to call him "the meditating bird." I fondled the idea that he was pondering world conditions, and when he failed to show up one morning I remarked to Sara, "His thinking over the situation has been too much for him; I'm afraid he has committed suicide!" But he hadn't, and when he returned next day we were relieved.

What I liked most about this silent long-necked and long-legged surveyor of the scene was his solitariness. He was definitely unsociable. When other birds arrived he departed. Now such a trait among us humans is deplored and denounced, but I do not share in such condemnation. We Americans are such a gregarious crowd, we cannot endure our own company. A loner is viewed with suspicion as though he were up to something. But eagles do not fly in droves, and there is much to be said for the few who have developed inner resources enough to enjoy solitude. Today we must have the TV on all day and carry a transistor radio lest we run out of noise. Entertainment is a top business because Americans must laugh or die; and really we do both, for we are laughing ourselves to death. A Chinese philosopher said, "Americans must be very unhappy, they laugh so much." There is deep wisdom behind that observation. One thinks of the old story about the nervous wreck who was advised by his doctor, "Go down to the theater and watch Grimaldi the clown. Everybody is holding his sides with merriment watching him perform." The sick patient replied, "But, doctor, you don't understand … *I am Grimaldi!*"

So my hat is off to "the meditating bird" and all his kind. Like sheep to the slaughter we follow blind leaders of the blind to destruction. We pay any price to be "in" with the current, the tide, the trend. Broad is the way that leads to death, and many travel it. We follow a multitude to do evil. We wear clothes we wouldn't want to be caught dead in because it is the style. Teenagers boast of being different, but there never was a generation more alike. The setup and spirit of this age have conspired against any man who would chart his own course. Four hundred false prophets bid Ahab and Jehoshaphat go up against Ramoth-gilead, and any lone Micaiah who dissents is in line for a diet of bread and water.

I believe the Lord is on the lookout for some "meditating bird" along the shores of these tragic times who does not live on second-hand canned goods from the popular thought-stores but gets his own direct from his own garden.

His loneliness will pay off like Daniel's when he is called in to read the handwriting on the wall at the feast of Belshazzar!

CHAPTER 15

Reclaimed

MANY years ago a friend gave me a walking stick. He had spent much time painstakingly carving it. It became my constant companion when I was a young preacher. Then came the day when I left my old home to return only now and then. The walking stick was was put in a closet, and there it stayed for over forty years. It never saw sunlight; and if it could have thought, it would have pined away in this solitary confinement for nearly half a century. "What have I done to deserve this?" it might have complained, and "why doesn't my master return and reclaim me?"

This spring I visited the old home one Sunday morning. I wanted to walk down an old road where I strolled as a boy. I remembered the old walking stick, and a search located it in that dark corner. I felt like David when he reclaimed Goliath's sword: "There is none like that; give it me" (1 Samuel 21:9). Down the old pasture trail we went, and I fancied that old walking stick was overwhelmed with ecstasy after forty years in prison and now set free. How would you feel to be outdoors in sunlight you hadn't seen since the late 20s?

A few days ago I had the old walking stick cleaned up and varnished, and now it is with me on a trip to the mountains. We've had a stroll this afternoon in the glory of early June and matchless scenery. The old stick must be doubly dumbfounded to find itself all spruced up and taking in the beauty of this favored spot. It must be saying, "This just can't be true. I must be dreaming. It's too good to last. Any minute I shall wake up and find myself in that dark closet!"

But it *is* true; and the secret is, the owner reclaimed a precious possession. There are souls in dark closets—once used and now disapproved as Paul feared he might be—forgotten and neglected. But other things than walking sticks can be reclaimed, given a new beauty, and brought into service far beyond their fondest dreams.

> Down in the human heart,
> Crushed by the tempter,
> Feelings lie buried that grace can restore;
> Touched by a loving heart,
> Wakened by kindness,
> Chords that are broken will vibrate once more.
> —Fanny Crosby

Do these lines meet the eye of some laid-aside Christian—perhaps even a minister—no longer useful because no longer usable? Ah, but the Master is looking for *you*. He would reclaim you and make you more useful than ever before. Remember, Simon Peter did his greatest work on his second chance.

There is one great difference between you and my walking stick. *You* can think and act. *You* can repent and call upon God. The Savior will hear you and give you a new glow within and without, and you will accompany your Master to places you never dreamed you would see.

We are in the reclamation business with our Lord. There are souls in dark closets all over this world who need to be found and furbished for the Master's use. What better business can engage us than a quest for castaways?

CHAPTER 16

Peace on the Parkway

ONE of the impressions of my boyhood years that time can never erase was the sinking of the *Titanic* in 1912. That luxurious liner went down on its first and last voyage. It was declared unsinkable, and the only thing it ever did was to sink.

Some of us felt that the *Titanic* disaster was the first in a long series of warnings, object lessons to remind proud man of his frailty and futility at the beginning of a century that was to see God humanized and man deified. The *Titanic* was the last word in shipbuilding and a plush testimony to the ingenuity of a generation just beginning to feel its oats and to boast of its inventions. It was unsinkable—and then it sank!

The sinking of the unsinkable! There was something weird, queer, uncanny about it all. From that day to this the unsinkable has been sinking. What couldn't happen has been happening. In the pre-teens of this century men thought that a world war was out of the question. We were too far advanced for that. But two years after the great ship went down, what couldn't happen did happen; and Germany, for all her smart progressiveness, plunged the world into war. And Hitler was still to come! Humanity turned out to be a savage with only a thin veneer of civilization. Progress was shown up for the grand illusion it is. Whoever thought we were on the way up had to learn (or did we?) what the Old Book said long ago: Man is not on his way up to a knowledge of God; he started with a knowledge of God and has been going the other way ever since. The trail from protoplasm to perfection was lost in the wilderness. For all the advance from Kitty Hawk to outer space we are gaining worlds and losing our souls. Those happy days of the Horatio Alger era were not a budding springtime ushering in a millenium, but the dying autumn before the chilling winds of winter. In 1912, who could have envisioned Hiroshima? The *Titanic* was indeed an object lesson. It was the sinking of the unsinkable, the beginning of the "impossible."

In 1912 we began to be heady with a new wine. Until a few years before, man had not been able to travel any faster than in the days of antiquity. Then all of a sudden he stepped on the gas. Soon there would be the airplane. It went to our heads, and one drink led to another until we have become sots, intoxicated with pride in our cleverness. At this writing we are in the delirium tremens stage. Our heads and hands have left our hearts far behind, and without God in our hearts we have arrived at worldwide insanity. By education and legislation we try to build heaven on earth, and what we have is more like hell. It started long ago when men said at Babel, "Let us build us a city and a tower, whose top may reach unto heaven; and let us make us a name" (Genesis 11:4). From that day to this, Babels have crashed around our ears; but we keep building them up again. Peace palaces in Geneva and the Hague stand as monuments to man's delusion that he can reach heaven from earth by his own devices. We are still obsessed with the notion that we can superimpose the kingdom of God on an unregenerate society. But every few years a new Babel crumbles. It is the *Titanic* all over again—the sinking of the unsinkable.

CHAPTER 17

Springtime in the Ozarks

A T this writing Sara and I are spending a few days in a lovely lodge on the Blue Ridge Parkway. I have been all over this land, and to me there is no spot more favored than the Western Carolina mountains. We found a place so peaceful that it took a little while to let our fever subside! The back porch looks out over pasture and rail fences and grazing cattle to the mountains beyond. The top of the hill nearby commands a breathtaking view of the valley below surrounded by lofty peaks; and in the valley is the cabin of a hardy pioneer who raised fourteen children eight miles from the nearest settlement. They had inner resources and self-reliance, unlike modern Americans who go frantic on a rainy afternoon if the television isn't working!

On one side we have serenity, on the other, sublimity. I haven't been so quiet since I was a boy on the back porch at home looking across the hills to Table Rock and Grandfather Mountain. It is so tranquil that as I watched the cattle ambling homeward—"the lowing herd winds slowly o'er the lea" (Gray's *Elegy*)—I could hear crickets chirping along the rail fence. There was an eerie silence—a serene sweetness that seemed like a dream and not reality. What a tonic for a tired preacher, weary from wrestling with the world, the flesh, and the devil in a world gone mad! I needed to get my bearings, to take stock, and make an inventory to "sanctify myself against tomorrow." I needed to pray, "Prepare me for what thou art preparing for me." I thought of the lines:

Give me the faith of the mountains, serene and sublime,
The deep-rooted joy of just living a day at a time,
Spurning the petty possessions the valley-folk buy

For the glory of glad, wind-swept spaces where earth meets the
    sky! —Author Unknown

I belong in a place like this, for I grew up in the hills. Maybe
I should never have left them! I was never meant to be a mixer.
Even as a boy preacher I often wished I could get out through
a pulpit window in the country church and escape to the woods
instead of meeting all those people.

I am glad to see so many campers on the roads. It is a good
sign that Americans are trying to get back to the woods. Some of
them are pretty awkward about it, but a little will do a lot of good.

At the beginning of a hiking path I read this warning: STAY
ON THE ESTABLISHED TRAILS. What a needed word for this generation that has lost its way! Indeed that is the meaning of "per-
plexity," one of the characteristics of the last days mentioned by
our Lord. We have left the old paths and the good way, and we
have no rest for our souls.

Any harassed preacher would do well to shut off his television set and find a back porch facing a pasture where he can hear
only the crickets. He may think for a few days that it will drive
him crazy. He will find out that he has already been crazy and is
just now returning to sanity.

I am thankful that Congressman Bob Doughton of North
Carolina and others had the vision to begin and build this
matchless parkway across the Blue Ridge Mountains where tired
travelers can rest their souls moving through this gorgeous glory
at a sensible speed (and without the torment of trying to pass a
truck every few miles). I have traversed almost the full length
of it in four visits this summer, and it will be my favorite escape
as long as I can make it. That it has been constructed and that
multitudes flock to it encourages me to believe that America has
not yet completely gone berserk.

There may yet be hope of recovery from the dementia of
these days.

CHAPTER 18

Fog in the Mountains

THESE lines are written in a mountain lodge on a foggy, drizzly morning with visibility zero. I came here to walk and meditate and catch some fresh inspiration, but one must take chances with that unpredictable factor—the weather. However, if by now I have not learned that seeking favored spots for special experiences is poor business, I should get a prize for stupidity.

I remember from my early years how one spring morning I took off to the woods quite sure that such a day would pay off in rich reward. Surely I would see a vision, dream a dream, come home laden with a store of fresh revelations. Instead, I sat under a tree, half asleep, while a pesky crow that spied me early made the morning miserable by announcing my presence to the neighborhood. It was a vain jaunt, and I gave up in disgust.

We cannot set the stage and work up a spiritual experience. One writer tells how he prayed one night in the garden of Gethsemane. Of all places, surely this would be the ideal setting for a rare meeting with God! Instead, it was a dull and most ordinary evening. I know that I have spent quiet moments in some of the loveliest spots in America, but my richest insights have not come in such settings. I have had my best thoughts in drab and difficult places. I keep remembering that Paul wrote his epistles not in a resort on the Mediterranean but in a Roman jail.

Elijah may have thought that at Horeb he would have some great new revelation. Horeb was Sinai where the Ten Commandments were given. But to Elijah God spoke only in a still small voice with routine orders to anoint Hazael and Jehu and Elisha. What we thought would be a Sinai often turns out to be a Horeb.

Have you reflected that our Lord used the wind—the changeable, unpredictable wind—as a symbol of the Spirit? Why did He choose such a figure that represents to us that which is most variable, less permanent, most difficult to chart or control? The weather prophets have wrestled with the wind for centuries, and their predictions fail as often as they succeed. Well, we cannot control the wind; but we can adjust to it, set up our windmills, and wait. The Spirit is not capricious and fitful, but God visits us in his own good time.

> We cannot kindle when we will
> The fire which in the heart resides,
> The Spirit bloweth and is still,
> In mystery the soul abides.
> —Matthew Arnold

But one thing we can do:

> … tasks in hours of insight willed
> Can be through hours of gloom fulfilled.

What matters most is faithfulness—in season and out, feel like it or not, vision or no vision.

Do not be a thrill-seeker, hunting favored spots where you may see an angel. You are as likely to have a fresh word from God in a cow pasture as on Pike's Peak. Moses did not meet God for his life call in a cathedral but in a bush. Get away to the lovely spot when you can—but don't count too heavily on it. You may go all the way to the mountain just to sit in a fog. High elevations do not guarantee holy inspiration. The big Bible conference in the mountains or by the lake may only tire you, and you may return home to meet the Lord in your room. One sometimes leaves the place of blessing going to look for one!

A trip to the mountains is not a failure if it rains and you are imprisoned in a dreary room. It is a failure if you do not rescue from the wreckage of your high expectations something more precious than anything a fog can spoil.

When Jacob met God in the ladder vision he called the place Bethel, "the house of God." When he returned to Bethel from his wanderings in Shechem he called it El-Bethel, "the God of the house of God." God had become more important than any place or experience. That is what Madame Guyon meant when she wrote:

> To me remains nor place nor time;
> My country is in every clime;
> I can be calm and free from care
> On any shore since God is there.

Wasn't expecting Vance to be Quoting Madame Guyon

?

CHAPTER 19

Weather Report

TODAY marks the official opening of winter by the calendar—which doesn't mean a thing. In this part of the country, winter borrows one month from autumn to start with and another month from spring to end with, which leaves seven months for spring, summer, and fall. Spring does well to last a month, and summer takes up most of autumn what with an extra chapter of Indian summer for good measure.

I have an allergy, antipathy, and aversion to winter. My favorite season is spring, the shortest of all. The first half of it is still mixed with the shivers of winter's stubborn departure. Then—just about the time things are getting right—summer arrives with a sizzling bang; and what started with shivers ends with sweat. Still I live for it, those blessed few days when the warblers come through and the blossoms stage their passing show—so slow to come and so soon to leave.

I would not want to be a meteorologist. Anything as uncertain as weather does not appeal to me. I do not like air travel for the same reason. The old trains managed to get through, but one morning fog can ground a monster jet and foul up a trip. I will never be able to understand why an age supposed to be intelligent should let passenger trains die when traffic has become a national horror. I used to think there would always be enough room in the sky for everybody; but now with planes stacked in airports awaiting clearance, even the wide blue yonder (no longer blue but black with pollution) is not wide enough.

I believe that the weather—along with everything else connected with this earth—was upset when sin broke up the bliss of Eden and the devil started his depredations. God controls everything in the last analysis, but Satan has considerable lee-way. He stirred up a great wind to destroy Job's children and churned up the Sea of Galilee with a storm. The fearful upheavals of hurricane, cyclone, tidal wave, lightning, hail, and torrent are disorders of a creation lost and ruined by the fall. I believe that just as the animals will one day pass from the rule of tooth and claw to the peace of the millennial kingdom, so will the elements subside in peace when our Lord reigns where'er the sun doth his successive journeys run. If the lion shall lie down with the lamb, shall not storm and tempest lose their savage fury in that blessed day?

I think we are utterly mistaken when we glibly attribute all natural disasters to Providence. "It's the Lord's weather," we piously assert; and indeed it is, in the sense that he is the Creator. But there is an evil spirit who is the prince of the power of the air. He may have a lot to do with hurricanes that seem demonic in their fury. Our Lord spoke of a crippled woman as one "whom Satan hath bound" (Luke 13:16), and Paul called his thorn in the flesh "the messenger of Satan" (2 Corinthians 12:7). Disease was credited to sin and the devil; and while Paul gloried in his infirmities, he did not glorify them. If sickness is due to the devil (if we trace it back far enough), storms can sometimes be classified in the same category.

At any rate, I'll make the best of winter and hope for spring. I cannot imagine any wintertime in the kingdom age and eternity. It will likely be more like springtime where everything is new and will never grow old. I do not anticipate the heat of summer, the sadness of autumn, the storms of winter then.

Every time I face a bone-chilling blast, I comfort myself with the reflection that one day I will have shivered through my last freeze.

5/29/2023
4:47 pm
Mom.

CHAPTER 20

Mississippi Mockingbird

I am preaching this week in a little Mississippi town near the Gulf. It is late September, and besides the noisy blue jays and the ever-present starlings, the only bird I can hear is the mockingbird. Somehow he sums up the spirit of days gone by in the dear old South and is a carry-over from those gentler times to the madhouse we live in today.

There is still a touch of simplicity and sweetness here not entirely spoiled by the ravages of progress. The Old South of my boyhood is gone, as industry has moved into the cotton fields, and the machine has wrought its devastation. More money— yes—more gadgets and gimmicks but, as Lewis Mumford said, "The South is wealthier in things money can buy but poorer in all things beyond price or purchase." The rat race leaves no time for meditation, for friendly conversation, for the unhurried living that once we knew. There is no time to live; we are frantic nervous wrecks kept going by pills, our years extended by drugs but drained of any real content by the demands of modernity.

What has happened to our way of life has happened also to our religion. The experts with their graphs and charts have moved into the church to organize, regiment, systematize, and correlate. I can remember when the churches went into big business, raising millions by "campaigns" after the pattern of money-raisers in the World War One Liberty Loan drives. Everything was done over in the new system. Report cards, banners, diplomas, seals, and statistics flourished as we moved toward the day of automation and computers. Christian doctrine was rethought, revised, and revamped; and today we behold a form of godliness without power—everything in the show window and very little on the shelves.

I cannot help the destruction of the Old South and the disappearance of its way of life. That is gone forever, and I am stuck with the new age. I shall endure it as best I can—a pilgrim in a strange land. But I will not be robbed of my old-time faith. That is up to me, and I shall maintain it however much the new school may smile at my "outmoded provincialism." It is still possible to live in this era of atoms and astronauts by simple faith in Jesus Christ, and there is no other way to keep one's sanity in this madhouse.

I believe the Bible is the Word of God. I believe Jesus Christ is the Son of God. I trust him as my Savior and confess him as my Lord. Some of us can recall the old country church revivals where sinners came to the "mourner's bench" to be converted. They were singing and saying, "I am coming to the cross, I am poor and weak and blind; I am counting all but dross, I shall full salvation find." And they found it. We still need to find it, and we shall find it where they found it. That childlike faith will carry us through this weird world just as it did our fathers. We cannot recover the old way of life they lived, but their Lord is sufficient even for these frantic days. We may have to ride jets and wade through psychedelic insanity, but the grace that has brought us safe thus far will lead us home.

The Mississippi mockingbirds have sung their way through many eras without changing their melody. Today they sound like their forbears back in the Civil War days, the Reconstruction, the early days of this century, the good days before the First World War. Splitting atoms and sending men to the moon mean nothing to them; they have not added a note either sweet or sour. Just so, the Christian ought to sing the same refrain as long ago; for though he must admit that he sees change and decay all around, he can confidently pray:

6/6/2023
3:57
.

O thou who changest not,
Abide with me!

CHAPTER 21

Saints and Stairs

I stood at the Lateran staircase in Rome where Martin Luther once crawled before God liberated him from seeking salvation by works of righteousness, freed him forever by that greatest of emancipation proclamations, "The just shall live by faith" (Romans 1:17). I watched a throng of poor souls laboriously toiling up the stairs, kneeling on each step for a prayer. Some could scarcely bend. For cripples it was an agony, and for all a pitiful exercise in futility. Millions today are still enslaved in hopeless bondage by which old Adam still seeks to merit divine approval in spite of that unmistakable word, "They that are in the flesh cannot please God" (Romans 8:8).

This multitude is not limited to any church. Baptists and Methodists and Presbyterians and many others are not climbing altar stairs on their knees, but nonetheless are seeking by "church work" and religious observances to secure forgiveness and justification. There is no difference in principle between stair-climbing penitents and some unsaved businessman who would secure his salvation with a fat check to some worthy cause.

It was from this *good that is not good enough* that God delivered Martin Luther. It detonated the charge that shook the church and started the Reformation. Today the apostles of compromise would have Martin Luther arrange a conference with the pope instead of a confrontation. Peaceful coexistence had not been heard of, and it was unthinkable to the great reformer that truth so bright should be mixed with error so dark. Two could not walk together if they were not agreed, and the same fountain could not send forth both bitter water and sweet. Luther knew nothing of that tolerance so popular today that would "suffer" Jezebel

53

in Thyatira, mingle righteousness with unrighteousness, light with darkness, and seek symphony between Christ and Belial. Of course the Reformation lapsed into state church-ism, never having come out completely from bondage. Protestantism still carries with it much that it should have dumped overboard, and the traveler is still hampered by his baggage.

As Christianity sinks lower, the more cathedrals, altars, ceremonies, vestments, pomp, and grandeur it accumulates. An abundance of lighted candles generally means that the power has been cut off! Was there ever a deader era than the Middle Ages for all its pageantry? Christianity really means a helpless babe in a manger, a cross, a grave in a garden, a prison in Rome, the deliverance of a lone miserable monk on a flight of stairs, a Wesley preaching in the fields. Its message is that the just shall live by faith. Fame and fortune and finery only slow its progress and clutter it with nonessentials.

There is, of course, a true upward climb, steps toward perfection; but we climb them not in order to be saved but because we *are* saved. We do not climb them to win acceptance with God; but, having won acceptance by the blood of the cross, we climb them to grow in grace and the knowledge of our Lord. Alas, too many of us get stuck at the start and spend our time staring up the steps instead of stepping up the stairs!

God grant us more saints of the staircase climbing the Jacob's ladder of an ever-ascending progress heavenward singing:

> I'm pressing on the upward way,
> New Heights I'm gaining every day.

CHAPTER 22

Red Light of the Centuries

NOTHING else so perfectly symbolizes the decline and fall of the world's greatest empire as does the Colosseum in Rome. The collapse of that mighty domain began when the Romans turned their attention from the Forum, where great issues were debated, to the Colosseum, where the sports events were held. Gibbon names five causes of Rome's demise: the breakdown of the home, taxation and doles, militarism, love of pleasure, and religious collapse. He also gave five reasons for Christianity's early success: inflexible and intolerant zeal, the doctrine of a future life, miraculous power, pure and austere morals, the union and discipline of the Christian republic. All of the causes of Rome's decay abound among us today while Christianity weakens and wanes on all counts.

At no point are we failing more than on morals. "Pure and austere" would hardly describe the ethics of most church members; and if anyone raises even a feeble protest he is branded "legalistic, reactionary, pharisaical, puritanical." But the early Christians would out-puritanize the Puritans if they lived today. "Modern" Christianity, with its permissiveness and indulgence, its compromise and acceptance of the mores of these last days, smiles in condescension and lofty disdain on any believer with a strict pattern of conduct today. "Legalism" is the usual word dismissing any insistence on discipline—if, indeed, there is any insistence. But an austere code of ethics is not legalism. Everything depends on the spirit behind it. The Pharisees were all letter and no spirit. If stern ethics grow out of love for God and a sincere desire to walk unblamably and unreprovably in his sight—that is not legalism. If a father disciplines his children because he loves them and seeks their best, endeavoring prayerfully to bring them up in the nurture and admonition of the Lord—that is not legalism. If a pastor is jealous over his flock with a godly jealousy, and holds a high standard for his people to the glory of God and the good of the church—that is not legalism. It is pharisaism only when Christian living is a set of dos and don'ts to feed one's self-righteousness. Love must be the motive, but not the cheap brand so popular today that says, for instance, that premarital sex is all right if the participants love each other.

Our lives, homes, churches, and nation disintegrate today because moral codes are not merely questioned but denied. It is a poor time to complain if some rare soul dares protest against our sellout to the world, the flesh, and the devil. It would be refreshing to meet someone who does have old-fashioned morals. The tribe is scarce and nearer extinction than whooping cranes. We would welcome a few Puritans.

The Colosseum holds warning for both church and state. We go the way of Rome, and we need a swing back from the Colosseum to the catacombs. The true church may be driven underground, and if so, may develop more vitality than is now evident above ground. We have come a long way since the church that once suffered in the arena now sits in the grandstand.

The Colosseum is a red light—a danger signal for the ages. God help us to heed its warning!

CHAPTER 23

Mamertine to Mausoleum

IT has been fairly well established that the Mamertine Prison in Rome was the apostle Paul's "study" when he wrote his letters to the Ephesians, Philippians, Colossians, Philemon, and the second letter to Timothy. It was not an ideal spot for writing. It could be described as "exceeding dark, unsavory, and able to craze any man's senses."

When one moves for a day amidst the pomp and pageantry of Romanism (I happened to get in on a public appearance of the pope at St. Peter's), the Mamertine offers the stark contrast of authentic Christianity. Here, and not in the cathedrals, chapels, and shrines is the true picture of the early church. Here the greatest of the apostles spent his closing days, not in robes of splendor, but awaiting in an old cloak Timothy was asked to bring that he might keep warm while he awaited decapitation outside the city walls.

Later on, Christianity overcame the Caesars and moved from the catacombs to the Colosseum. Constantine made it fashionable, and paganized it under the pretext of Christianizing paganism. The church married the world and has never recovered from that unholy wedlock.

Today comfortable congregations sing on Sunday mornings:

> Faith of our fathers, holy faith,
> We will be true to thee till death.

Most of them are not true enough to get back for the evening service!

They also sing:

> Our fathers, chained in prisons dark
> Were still in heart and conscience free.
> How sweet would be their children's fate
> If they, like them, could die for thee!

But most of them do not know what they are singing. (If they did honesty would choke them.) We have come a long way from Mamertine Prison, and now we dwell in Laodicea, "rich and increased with goods and needing nothing" (Revelation 3:17). But the heart of Christianity beats strongest in prisons, not in palaces—the catacombs, and not in the Colosseum. The trail of Christian history runs from Mamertine to mausoleum, and we are nearing the mausoleum. We have moved into the upper brackets and we socialize with the jet set. We almost apologize for our forebears, like Mr. Newly-rich referring to his country relatives. Mamertine Prisons do not fit well into our picture.

True Christianity is in as sharp contrast to our modern churchanity as Paul's prison to the ecclesiastical pomp of Rome. If there is to be a resurgence of it in these evil days, it will likely begin in circumstances just as lowly as the dungeon of its beginnings. Revivals have never started in cathedrals but in camp meetings. Paul in prison does not compare favorably with Nero in his palace. It has been pointed out, however, that now we call our dogs Nero and our boys Paul!

Christianity tends to move from Mamertine to mausoleum. We have a name to be alive today but we are dead.

Better return to dungeon, fire, and sword!

CHAPTER 24

Unimpressed in Athens

FROM my table in the hotel dining room here in Athens, I look out tonight to the nearby Acropolis where the Parthenon—majestic even in its ruins—stands resplendent in the floodlights. Even in its desolation, it speaks across the centuries and tells us again that the only thing we learn from history is that we learn nothing from history. I cannot escape the weird and eerie feeling that from this mountain there looks down upon me the ghost of a civilization that has never been equalled since. Yet it failed because it did not know God.

Greece was already a Roman province when Paul visited it, but the glory had only begun to fade. Yet this little Jew, aflame with one obsession, was not impressed by statues, by art, by the culture of that day. He bore not the slightest resemblance to the average American tourist. No ohs and ahs escaped his lips. What moved him was their ignorance—the last charge anybody else would have leveled against Athens! But ignorance it was because they did not know God. When a man does not know God, he is an ignoramus—an educated ignoramus, maybe—but as our Lord put it, if one does not know the Scriptures nor the power of God, he lives in error.

Today evangelical Christianity is more impressed by Athens than was Paul. Some of our leaders lament our lack of art appreciation. We are exhorted to comb the hayseed out of our hair and brush up on esthetics. They tell us that we must be conversant with the culture of our time. Some of the brethren bewail our dullness as though we were a flock of yokels as ill at ease in Athens as farmers come to town.

Vital religion was never lower than in the heyday of great cathedrals and medieval culture. The church never had less dynamics than when she had most dramatics. The farther we get from reality the nearer we draw to make-believe. Simulation supplants actuality. The great revivals did not break out in universities and art colonies. The Wesleyans, the Moravians, the Puritans were not connoisseurs touring galleries and museums. Not many wise, mighty, and noble have been called; and gospel movements that have shaken the world have begun with plain people. No spiritual earthquakes have been registered on the seismographs of the intelligentsia.

We Christians could spend our time better than in "getting with it" in cultural appreciation. We had better be concerned about American altars to the Unknown God. The country is full of them. And there are those who would put our Lord alongside Plato or Socrates or Buddha, just one more statue in the museum of antiquity.

We need more Pauls with burning heart aglow with zeal to tell our modern Athenians that we know the "Unknown God," ready to preach as he did on Revelation, Resurrection and Repentance. We are too easily impressed by the phony grandeur of our time.

Amidst all the fallen statues and broken pillars of the Acropolis there is a bronze tablet on which is recorded Paul's Mars' Hill sermon in Greek. How eloquently that reminds us that heaven and earth shall pass away but not God's Word! Paul has outlasted all the glory of Greece. He had known Jesus Christ and that spoiled him for everything else!

> He had seen the face of Jesus;
> Tell him not of aught beside;
> He had heard the voice of Jesus
> And his soul was satisfied.

CHAPTER 25

The Deaf Generation

ANCIENT ACOUSTICS

IN Caesarea we saw an outdoor theatre, not an amphitheatre, but a semicircular stone auditorium. From the back row we could hear our leader speak in conversational tones from the platform. Moreover, he told us that a larger theatre in Ephesus that could hold twenty-four thousand was constructed centuries ago with the same marvelous acoustics. All this in a day when in my travels all over America I have had congregations of a hundred or so complain that they could not hear in a tiny church! Larger edifices wrestle continually with the problem. All our experts somehow cannot come up with the acoustics of antiquity!

How many times have listeners in little auditoriums lamented that hearing was bad only a few yards from the pulpit! Could it be that we slaves of our own devices have become so accustomed to hearing aids of all sorts that we imagine we cannot hear without them? We limp on our crutches, and if the amplifier does not work "hearing we hear not" (Matthew 13:13).

Once I listened to the veteran evangelist, Gipsy Smith. He was a preacher of the old days and abhorred all new devices. I thought I could not hear him; and when he asked if any of us were having trouble about it, I raised my hand. "You're not listening!" was his reply. Could it be that, conditioned as we are to mechanical aids, we just think we cannot hear the preacher?

And of course, those dear souls who come to church early to get a back seat could move up closer and fill that empty lumberyard of ten rows of seats right in front of the pulpit. But they never do, yet still insist that they cannot hear!

"Ears that hear not." "He that hath ears to hear, let him hear" (Mark 4:9). Ears to hear! All of us are equipped with ears, but hearing is another matter. We hear and we do not hear. Our ears catch vocal sounds emanating from the pulpit, but the message escapes us. We hear (after a fashion) what the minister says, but our Lord said, "Let him hear what the Spirit saith" (Revelation 2:7). Of course sometimes the preacher is not saying what the Spirit says, and if we listened ever so well there would be no word from God. Or the trouble may be not with the transmitter but with our receiver! There is a preparation to *hear* the sermon as well as a preparation to deliver the sermon.

We live now in an ear-splitting age of amplified dissonance, and some think the next generation will have to be equipped with hearing aids. The more our eardrums are bombarded with demonic waves of music (which is not music but only an excuse for not being able to make music), the deafer our souls will be.

Something has gone wrong with our hearing—both physically and spiritually. We are not going to correct it by clever devices. We must get at the cause. We need to do something about *how* we hear as well as *what* we hear. There is famine of the hearing of the Word of God—a famine because in some quarters it is not being preached and in others because our ears are not tuned and trained to hear it.

God grant us more Samuels who can say, "Speak, Lord, for thy servant heareth" (1 Samuel 3:9)!

CHAPTER 26

From Athens to Corinth

SARA and I rode from Athens to Corinth along the oleander-lined highway by the Aegean Sea through vineyards and olive groves. A lot of water has run under the bridge since the apostle Paul came from his Mars Hill experience with firm resolve to know nothing among the Corinthians but Christ crucified. I do not know how he made the trip. Certainly it was not in an air-conditioned coach such as we used for our journey. He came from Athens, the center of a civilization that set standards for all subsequent time. He came to Corinth, a city whose name had become a synonym for the lowest and vilest in wickedness. In either city there was but one answer to all evil: the preaching of the cross—which is to the world foolishness, moronic—but to all who receive it, the power and wisdom of God.

Bible students have differed as to Paul's speech in Athens. Some have contended that he made a mistake in adapting his message to the Athenians, and that he therefore resolved never again to aim at the ear of the intellectuals. I do not think he failed; but for many a minister, the road from Athens to Corinth is a long one, and some never make it. Too many sermons today sound like a pitiful effort to please a generation that spends its time in nothing else but to tell or hear some new thing. When our Lord expounded the Scriptures it caused heartburn, but we have come all the way from heartburn to ear itch. Paul had no time to waste on Athenians. He went back to Lystra, where they dragged him out of town, supposing him to be dead; but he never returned to Athens.

It is a long road for a minister from Athens to Corinth. Today we like to be recognized among the literati, and we are urged to make our message relevant and contemporary with the Now. To renounce all scholarly attempts to please the Athenians, to resolve once and for all to preach a message which is to the world foolishness (and therefore makes the preacher to the world a fool), that is not a cheap experience. It brands the preacher an outdated provincial, a throwback, out of step with the times. Paul calls it "the foolishness of God" and "the weakness of God" (1 Corinthians 1:25). That means that the messenger must be a fool for Christ's sake, and that God's strength is made perfect in weakness.

The aspiring seminary graduate will be tempted to adjust to Athens. Gradually we are being brainwashed with a new universalism that conjures up a gospel which is a mulligan stew of all religions. A book on missions says that the early apostles may have been mistaken when they insisted that there is no other name but Christ whereby we must be saved. Such exclusiveness, we are told, does not make for dialogue. Why should it? There is nothing to dialogue about! If no man comes to God but by Jesus Christ, that settles it. Why get out new maps offering a selection of highways when all others are ways that seem right unto a man but end in death?

Many a minister needs to journey from Athens to Corinth. It makes no sense to this age, and trying to popularize it is casting pearls before swine and holy things to dogs. We might as well try to explain nuclear physics to a wooden Indian in front of a cigar store.

Christ crucified and risen can never be made acceptable to this world. He does not await our approval. We must come to him on his terms. But he that cometh he will in no wise cast out.

CHAPTER 27

The Miracle of Israel

FROM the balcony of my hotel room on the edge of Tel Aviv I watch early this morning the Mediterranean waves play along the shore. Everywhere I behold the miracle of Israel back in the land: the thriving city, the desert blossoming as the rose, the fabulous transformation of rocks and rubble into orange groves, opulent farms, and the phenomenon of a people gathered from many lands back to the homeland (which someone has described as "not a melting pot but a pressure cooker!").

Thirty years ago a college president said, "Israel will never return to Palestine. Jews love the cities where they can make money. They would never go back to that rock pile." Back at the turn of the century some Bible scholars saw Israel's return when it was as unlikely (to quote Dr. Carl Henry) as a Swiss navy. They put it into the Scofield Bible, which is laughed at in some circles. They were right about it, as they were about the rise of Russia as a commanding figure in the last days. True, Israel is back in unbelief; but it is there, and the stage is set.

Anyone who can sit where I sit this morning and not be moved as he watches Scripture being fulfilled would have to be blind in both eyes and bereft of his brains. Such ignorance abounds even in church circles, and it is that wilful ignorance Peter wrote about (see 1 Peter 1:14). Here is the reassembling of God's chosen people promised to the Old Testament prophets. God made a promise that must be fulfilled. It cannot be transferred to the church as some have believed. There is no other nation on earth comparable to this little country that lives in a sort of desperation. They must win or else—there is no second choice. Every day is an emergency, every citizen is ready to die for his homeland. James Reston wrote: "These people have acted as if the life of the nation was everything and their personal lives were incidental."

What impresses me most is not this miracle *in* Israel but the miracle *of* Israel itself. Let it not be forgotten that Israel was a miracle to begin with! Isaac was born of aged parents and we read, "In Isaac shall thy seed be called" (Genesis 21:12; Romans 9:7). Likewise, the church began with a miracle—the virgin birth of our Lord—and every Christian begins with the new birth. In all three cases there is a miracle.

Something of the utter dedication and desperation that characterizes Israel ought to mark the church—the purchased people of God. Israel has maintained her identity century after century in many lands speaking many languages and now dwells in her native land, speaking Hebrew, her native tongue. Never assimilated but always different, how like that the church should be! Alas, we are so anxious to "identify" that we have merged into the world around us. The salt is so mixed with the elements of this age that it has lost its savor. We are to infiltrate the world but the world has assimilated us. When are we going to learn to be *in* it but not *of* it? When will we regain our pilgrim character as exiles and aliens on the earth? In our well-intentioned identification with the world, we do not mold it—it molds us. We are not to be isolated but insulated, moving in the midst of evil but untouched by it.

So I wish this morning here in Israel that we could learn a lesson from this compact little land so utterly consumed by its magnificent obsession. No other nation could have defeated a ring of foes in a few days. If the church could stand as resolutely, no confederation of men or demons could defeat such an overwhelming minority.

And we could say like that old captain when he was told that his little band was surrounded, "Don't let one of them escape!"

SO HOW DO THEY GLOSS OVER MIARY ?

CHAPTER 28

View from a Window

A S I stood one morning at my hotel window on the Mount of Olives in Jerusalem I was overwhelmed by a staggering thought. Before me within the confines of my window lay the greatest view on earth. Here in dusty old Jerusalem, looking like a ghost town in the early morning, is concentrated more history than can be seen at any other spot in this world. Amidst all these stones and rubble, the most important events of all time have transpired. Here is compacted the history of Israel from Abraham on Moriah to the present exciting day. Before me reigned David and Solomon and all the kings of Judah. Here Isaiah and Jeremiah prophesied.

But greater than all, within the framework of this window God's Son died and rose, ascended to the Father, and here he will come again. Here the Holy Spirit came and the church began. All other windows on earth look out on nothing like that. How any man with even the feeblest comprehension can look on such a stage and not be overwhelmed by what happened and what will happen here is beyond me. I have not recovered, and I hope I will never recover from this view from a window.

Do not forget that all the dusty ruins spread before me bear witness to the prophecy of a rejected Messiah: "Behold, your house is left unto you desolate" (Matthew 23:38). *Desolate!* What word can better say what you see from this window? This old city has been invaded and captured and sacked and pillaged, destroyed and rebuilt. Three temples have risen and disappeared. Shishak and Sennacherib, Nebuchadnezzar, Antiochus Epiphanes, Pompey and Titus, the Persians, the Saracens, the Turks, the Crusaders, Saladin, the Ottomans, General Allenby all have left their footprints. Yet Jerusalem has survived in its desolation awaiting the Messiah whose right it is to reign. Gory is its past, glorious is its future! Because of all it has been, all it is, and all it will be, you can never see anything like it from any other window on earth.

This is the hub of God's history within history. The historians of this age do not know that history so they see no special significance in the view from my window. But if God really sent his Son to this world to meet the problem of its sin—and thereby meet all other problems—then here is the hub of history, for here he accomplished his purpose. I believe he did it; and I rest my soul, my life, my all upon him and what happened here within the compass of my window. I came a long way to see this view, but what a distance he traveled to provide it!

I have read often about "A Window on the World." Alas, a window on this poor world today reveals only chaos, misery, and despair, no matter where you stand. To an ordinary tourist, a window view of Jerusalem affords only a picture of a beaten and ravaged old city, battered by the centuries. A good travel guide can make it more interesting as he reels off a rundown of its past. But there is another guide sent down from heaven, one called alongside to help the Christian. We call him the Holy Spirit. Let him stand with you at a window overlooking Jerusalem, and you will see and feel what is hidden to all natural men who receive not the things of the Spirit of God for they are spiritually discerned.

What you behold from my window in Jerusalem depends on your guide!

CHAPTER 29

Bethlehem

FROM a distant mountain I first viewed Bethlehem. Through my mind ran those lines of Phillips Brooks inspired by his visit to the birthplace of our Lord:

> The hopes and fears of all the years
> Are met in thee tonight.

He was right. It stirs my soul to reflect that all the ecstasies and the agonies, the dreams and the despair of this poor wretched world today as in all ages past are met by what happened in one little town centuries ago. Here God sent the answer to man's need in a baby born of a peasant woman, born in a stable. How different from the way we would have planned it! It is a good thing we had nothing to do with it. Even to this day we spoil the significance of his birth and death and resurrection by tradition, shrines, pomp, and ceremony. What would he say about all these costly edifices built around spots where he may or may not have been? The commercialization, the hucksters, the fanfare, these only disgust the reverent heart. But from a distance we can see Bethlehem and know that somewhere there the hopes and fears of all the years were met long ago.

The baby was made known to the shepherds—the working class; to the wise men—the student class; to Simeon and Anna—the worshiping class. He is still made known to us in our work, our study, our worship. But somehow his coming is still lost in vague mistaken notions about "peace on earth, good will to men." The average Christmas card does not come near suggesting what he really came to do. He came to save us from our sins; and now,

69

centuries later, we still will not admit that our real trouble is sin. Poverty, ignorance, yes, but not sin. Does anybody dare to suggest to Congress or to the United Nations that this is the root of all our troubles?

Something was done about sin at Bethlehem long ago. Until we face that, all the pretty pictures of watching shepherds and singing angels and the magi and Joseph and Mary wearing halos are just window dressing for an empty window. Phillips Brooks went on to write:

> O holy child of Bethlehem,
> Descend on us, we pray;
> Cast out sin and enter in,
> Be born in us today.

All the celebration of the nativity is a waste of time unless and until the Savior is born in our hearts. That calls for a miracle. Sin has gotten us into more trouble than all our science can get us out of. It calls for divine intervention, and that is what happened in Bethlehem.

It was a master stroke of the devil to mix this blessed event with pagan holidays and heathen orgies until today the Christmas worshiper is bewildered in a hodgepodge of fact and fancy. Anything to obscure the real business of our Lord and true meaning of the Word becoming flesh to dwell among us! Truly Satan has blinded our minds lest the light of the glorious gospel shine upon us! Anything to keep us from facing our sins and the need of a Savior!

It is about time we rediscovered Bethlehem!

CHAPTER 30

Bethel and El-Bethel

WHEN the leader of our touring party asked his Bible class, "What did Melchizedek have in his hand when Abraham met him?" a very bright boy facetiously answered, "Postcards." When a flock of American travelers meets a band of Arab souvenir peddlers, the pandemonium is complete. Of all places, Jerusalem should be most conducive to reflection and meditation, but I have not encountered many tourists seeking solitude. "We didn't come all these miles and spend all this money just to sit and think," they tell us. They certainly do not sit, and I have a suspicion that neither do they think. After you've seen the sights and taken the pictures and bought the trinkets and written the cards, when would you or could you meditate? The average American is not disposed toward or equipped for anything but several mad weeks that will require several months to get over.

Jerusalem is a maze of shrines and mosques and sanctuaries, a labyrinth of traditional sites where this may have happened or that could have taken place. When Jacob went back to Bethel it was renamed El-Bethel, the God of the House of God. God was more important than any place. Jerusalem is long on Bethels and short on El-Bethel these days. I believe it was in the providence of God that we should not know for certain the exact location of Calvary and the open tomb. The shrine would have become more important than the Savior. God dwells not in temples made with hands. Our Lord made clear to the Samaritan woman the true meaning of worship—neither in Jerusalem or Samaria but in spirit and in truth.

The seeker after God discovers before he travels far that his most precious experiences are not found in what would seem

71

most propitious places. I have sought exalted moments in favored spots but usually in vain. I have never been more stupid and dull than in circumstances calculated to translate me to third heaven. On the other hand, it has been in some unromantic place and at some unlikely time that heaven came down and glory filled my soul. Jacob had his greatest vision in a strange land with a stone for a pillow. That pillow became a pillar; and when we have been long on the road, we shall look back to see that the markers of our best experiences were set up in dark and dangerous places, not in idyllic scenes and celebrated shrines. It was on the backside of the desert that Moses came to the mountain of God.

When and to whom did our Lord say that he would make himself real? Not in ecstatic visions or in some great meeting—but to them that love him and keep his commandments (John 14:21). Doesn't sound very exciting, does it? It is on the ordinary, everyday road of obedience that we really get acquainted with the Lord.

It has been said that nothing is more harmful to a deeper Christian experience than too many so-called Christian experiences. We major on Bethels; but in bounding from one Bethel to another we accumulate a lot of Bethels but only an occasional, irregular knowledge of El-Bethel.

CHAPTER 31

Stranger in Galilee

I sit this morning on the porch of my room overlooking the Sea of Galilee. The sun has just risen. The trees around are full of singing birds. I see a fisherman in his boat just as the Lord and his disciples must have looked long ago. I have been reading about him in his appearances here from the day when he called his first disciples to the touching interview with Peter after his resurrection. Whether he is calling Peter for the first time or reinstating him when he was temporarily not a discile in Mark 16:7 ("Go ... tell his disciples *and Peter*"), the Sea of Galilee is the setting. Here he gave the parables of Matthew 13 and the Bread of Life discourse of John 6. It was upon these shores that the multitude pressed upon him for healing.

There were two favored spots in the life of our Lord—the mountain and the sea. Paul was a man of the cities; and that was well, for the spreading of the gospel required such a man in the great centers of crowded humanity. But our model, our example, set us the perfect pattern and pace in the gait of Galilee. He arose long before day, found a solitary place, and there prayed. He found both time and place for communion with God, and so must we. Both are hard to come by today in this rat race—this madhouse we misnamed progress. If you find such a spot for solitude you must pay a price. The places grow fewer and harder to reach, and a minister must devise ways and means to find his hiding place unknown to telephones and committees and those pests who steal his time to no good purpose at all. And time is the scarcest commodity ever. Crowded calendars filled with appointments made in church offices leave no time for God. Much of

73

our "church work" could be done—and maybe is done—without the Holy Spirit.

William Law wrote, "Who am I to lie folded up in a bed of a morning when the farmers have already gone about their work ... and I'm so far behind with my sanctification!" His was an uncrowded age. What would that good man say in the insane asylum of this century!

This morning by the Sea of Galilee restores my soul. All my life I have been a rebel, and have sought in countless spots all over America to find here and there a bit of Galilee. This morning I am back at the source where it all started. One can look out and almost expect to see Peter and Andrew, James and John washing their nets. And when life grows turbulent we do not forget that Satan stirred up a storm even on these placid waters, but he was no match for the Lord of the weather who walked the boisterous waves. Not even the Sea of Galilee is immune, and into your most peaceful haven the fury may break—but the Lord will see you "toiling in rowing" (Mark 6:48) and will walk the waves to your relief. If he bids you come to him on the water—make a start. Peter did not walk far on the water, but he walked farther than any other of us has ever gone! And even if you sink, the Lord will reach you with his hand.

"But when the morning was now come, Jesus stood on the shore" (John 21:4). He still waits on a Galilean shore to call disciples—to reinstate the backslider. He still walks Galilean waters in time of storm. He still invites you to the "gait of Galilee" in these times of tumult.

God forbid that he be to you the stranger of Galilee!

CHAPTER 32

The Last Battlefield

TEDDY Roosevelt said, "We stand at Armageddon, and we battle for the Lord." Douglas MacArthur said at the surrender of Japan, "If we do not now devise some more equitable system, Armageddon will be at our door." The word has taken on many meanings in many minds. The interpretation of it has ranged from a mere symbol of the final clash between good and evil to detailed programs of extreme literalists who read in or read out of the record more than it contains.

I rode through the world's last battlefield today. No one with any degree of Bible understanding can visit the Valley of Esdraelon without a sense of being where strange things have happened and where strange things lie ahead. Here Barak defeated the Canaanites when "the stars in their courses fought against Sisera" (Judges 5:20). Here King Saul was defeated and died. Here King Josiah was slain. Here General Allenby defeated the Turks and was given the title Viscount Allenby, Marshal of Megiddo. Dr. George Adam Smith wrote:

"What a plain! upon which not only the greatest empires, races and faiths, East and West, have contended, but each has come to judgment and men felt there was fighting from heaven."

Israel is the crossroads of the world and the center of history. Mighty forces converge on the Mediterranean today. One would have to be blind and brainless to see no significance in the confrontation of the communist colossus and the free world. In the midst of it all lies tiny Israel. God's chosen people are back in their land, but the future is not as lovely as some imagine. Antichrist will be accepted first before Israel looks on him whom they have pierced and receives the true Messiah. Our Lord said, "If another comes in my name, him ye will receive" (see John 5:43). The time of Jacob's trouble is still future. The final clash—however one may line up the participants—will be at Armageddon. A look at the valley is enough; there is room here for the battle of all battles. I am glad I have had a preview. I don't expect to be here when the holocaust comes, but I like to know where it will be.

Armageddon is God's answer to all the progressivists who dream of a new age ushered in by legislation, education, social reformation. That dawn will break only after a mighty confrontation—not a conference of diplomats. My Lord is not coming back to negotiate. He will put all his enemies under his feet. All the way through the New Testament there is the message of final judgment: thrones, fire and brimstone, a great gulf fixed, a bottomless pit and a lake of fire, earthquakes and falling stars, and men praying for rocks and mountains to hide them from the wrath of God. History does not end in idyllic storybook form. It comes to a head in a valley of slaughter. But it does not end at Armageddon. It comes to its climax—not with the *Alas!* of a fallen Babylon, but with the *Alleluia!* of the redeemed—new heavens and a new earth.

I am glad to have had a look at the last battlefield. Armageddon is more than vivid imagery. It is grim reality, and some who laughed at its meaning a few years ago are beginning to sober up a bit. Some old-timers are coming into their own, and Bible prophecy is becoming respectable in some quarters.

Some who once laughed now stand in sombre awe in the presence of this silent valley quietly awaiting that awful day after which we "ain't gonna study war no more."

CHAPTER 33

Prophets—Then and Now

O N this, my last day in Jerusalem, although I must arise before day tomorrow to fly to Switzerland, I must also forego my afternoon rest and spend these precious hours on the Mount of Olives. From this outlook—away from American tourists and Arab peddlers—I survey all the land around. Below me lie Jerusalem and Bethany. Bethlehem is not far away. Here Isaiah preached to a generation with ears that heard not and eyes that did not see. Here Jeremiah wished that his eyes were fountains of tears that he might weep for his people. And here the Prophet of all prophets cried:

"O Jerusalem, Jerusalem, thou that killest the prophets and stonest them that are sent unto thee, how often would I have gathered thy children together, even as a hen gathereth her chickens under her wings, and ye would not!" (Matthew 23:37).

In this breeding place of prophets one is moved to enquire, Where is there a John the Baptist today to call men to repentance before Jesus returns just as that forerunner did before the Messiah first appeared? We live again in a day that kills prophets and persecutes the messengers of God. It is done with more finesse than when the Baptist's head was brought in a serving platter. It is done by the clever conniving of religious politicians just as the greatest of prophets was crucified by the religious leaders of his time. His is the fate of all who bug the status quo and call men back from performance to experience, from letter to spirit, from ritual to righteousness.

There are no salaries, no retirement benefits, no comfortable sinecures in the ecclesiastical setup for such prophets as prophesied here. Just as Isaiah and Ezekiel were told that their congregations would hear but not heed, so we are told in these last days to "preach the Word" and immediately informed that our listeners will not endure sound doctrine (having moved from the heartburn of the Emmaus Road to the ear itch of the end-time).

From here I look across to the high mountain I climbed yesterday where Herod lived in splendor centuries ago. Herod is gone and the palace is in ruins.

> The tumult and the shouting dies;
> The captains and the kings depart;
> Still stands thine ancient sacrifice,
> An humble and a contrite heart.
> —Rudyard Kipling

He who would call the church back to that brokenness that leads to blessedness must have a broken heart himself. He is not ready to say with Isaiah, "Here am I" (Isaiah 6:8) until first he has cried, "Woe is me!" (v. 5). No amount of facts in his head can compensate for lack of fire on his lips.

Jonah, the weakest of Old Testament prophets, had the biggest results statistics-wise, while Isaiah, prince of prophets, had no converts that anybody knows about. This is not to disparage results or justify no results, but heaven has not yet installed our computer system for tabulating prophetic success and failure. Almighty God does not choose his prophets according to recommendations from divinity schools. The God who passed up all the other sons of Jesse to choose the only one who was not even named among the prospects is not dependent on talent scouts.

He knows who and where the true prophet is and will find him and a place for him. Whether his listeners will hear or forbear is incidental, but they shall know that a prophet hath been among them.

CHAPTER 34

The Valley and the Mountain

FROM my window high in the Intercontinental Hotel in Geneva I look out this lovely afternoon on two impressive sights: the old League of Nations building (now called United Nations) nearby and Mont Blanc far in the distance. The two impressions they create are radically opposed to each other. The League of Nations building symbolizes a vain hope and an impossible dream of world peace through the conniving of men. Mont Blanc, like the Jungfrau we saw this morning, towers as a figure of stability and permanence in a world gone mad.

I remember the days following the First World War when Woodrow Wilson came to Paris to sit with Lloyd George, Clemenceau, and Orlando intent on fashioning an enduring peace. Wilson died a broken man, and the Second World War made havoc of all the well-laid plans of men to create a warless world. These imposing buildings are only a monument to the ignorance of brilliant men concerning God's purposes in history. They will not believe that only Jesus Christ can bring peace to this world, and that only when he comes again. Such a solution cannot even be mentioned in the United Nations!

Whether The Hague or Geneva or New York, man builds his temples in vain; for world peace does not come by politics and diplomacy.

It is encouraging to lift one's eyes from these monuments to man's ignorance to a mighty peak that rears its snowy shoulders high above the din and tumult. Mount Blanc was here before Geneva was built and will be here when Geneva is gone. I think God set up the mountains to remind us valley dwellers of earth that there is someone higher who looks upon our little doings in silent majesty. I remember reading about a poor factory worker who used to climb a mountain each evening after his day's work was done just to get away from the grime and the gloom and the grind and remind himself that he had a soul. Mountains have an upward pull, and the Almighty has graciously created an ample supply lest we succumb to a valley existence.

We do not decry what man has done in his valleys. Geneva is a beautiful city. The League of Nations building is a stately edifice. But over it all tower the Alps in their sublimity, and they make us look like the pygmies we are. Last week I looked out over Jerusalem, and there, too, the mountains have silently watched centuries come and go, kingdoms rise and fall. The valley needs the mountain to balance the picture. We cannot build three tabernacles and stay on the mountain, for we are needed in the valley. But we shall do poor work in the valley if we do not lift our eyes to the heights.

Nothing is more important than to keep our perspectives in order. Man is so constituted that he tends to spend all his time either in the valley or on the mountain. He becomes a lowlander without lifting his eyes upward. I have read of an old hillbilly who lived close to a great mountain. A new road was made that led clear to the summit. One day the old mountaineer was taken to the top to see the breathtaking view below. His comment was, "Just think, I've lived here all my life with all this to see—and I almost missed it!" But there are some who want to stay on the crest away from the world and its needs. Our Savior had the double perspective—he got away from the valley to the mountain and he returned from the mountain to the valley.

Unless we are equipped with bifocals, we shall see only mountains shrouded in mist and men as trees walking. God had more in mind than mere geography when he mixed the peaks and the plains.

CHAPTER 35

Getting Used to Beulah Land

IF there is anywhere a lovelier spot than where this afternoon finds me, I do not know where it is. The balcony of my hotel room looks out on Lake Lucerne surrounded by the majestic Alps raising their snow-covered shoulders through the clouds. A man cannot sit here and ascribe what he sees to a mere concourse of atoms. If he could, then his soul has long since died within him. Nor can I see how anyone in this cheap and tawdry day can view what I now behold and not feel rebuked for his littleness in the presence of such sublimity.

How many of the throng walking the lakefront below really see this glory I do not know. Some do not see it because they did not come here to see it. They came for fun and pleasure, and that does not gear a man for this. Others are accustomed to it, since they live here and the scenes are familiar. Throngs of jaded tourists hurry through, but it is only another item on their crowded calendar. And there are multitudes who have no eyes to see it.

For pretty much the same reasons, men do not see the glory of God in Jesus Christ. Certainly men who are out for the pleasures of this world are blind to higher things. And even Christians grow so accustomed to sacred matters that, as with Uzzah (2 Samuel 6) in the Old Testament, the ark becomes only a box and familiarity breeds contempt.

People who live here in Lucerne get used to it. So do men become so accustomed to the things of God that they lose the sense of awe. They play marbles with diamonds. What overwhelms the new Christian becomes to old Christians customary and ordinary. People who live near great sights seldom see them, while thousands come from afar to see them. I am sure that is true in Lucerne. I lived in a historic old city for five years and never saw some things a multitude of visitors came long distances to admire.

For whatever reason, it is a sad day when we lose the wonder and accept the glory of the gospel as a matter of course. I cannot sleep late here tomorrow for I want to see Lucerne by the dawn's early light. Would that we rose with as much anticipation to find new vistas in the Word of God on our tables, a wonderland beside which all the grandeur of earth fades away!

The Christian is headed for heaven, but even now he may dwell in Beulah Land. He needs only to possess his possessions. More wonderful than any sight this earth affords is the life hid with Christ in God. There are mountains to cross and rivers to ford and quiet resting places. It is morning now, and my view of the Alps is obscured by rain and fog; and so it is sometimes in the world of the spirit. But we know that the Alps are still there and that the sun will shine again. The darkness may veil his lovely face, but we rest in his unchanging grace. There are sights yet to be seen on my visit to Switzerland, and there remaineth yet very much land to be possessed in Canaan. It is not enough to read travel books and tourist guides. Like Caleb of old we would say, "Give me this mountain!" (Joshua 14:12).

Switzerland and Beulah Land are great—if you don't get used to them!

CHAPTER 36

Where Lies Your Heart?

IN Westminster Abbey I walked by the tombs of kings and queens and other celebrities of centuries past, passed inscriptions honoring great names of England's long history. This musty old mausoleum of the ages lists the great and near-great, the famous and some infamous. Most of them meant little to me, but beneath the floor of the chapel lies the body of David Livingstone under an epitaph on which countless thousands have walked! I had been told that most visitors to the chapel walk around the inscription, but nowadays we have a generation that has heard little and cares less about the great missionary whose heart is buried in Africa while the rest of his body reposes here.

These notables interred here mean little as such in the sight of God. I am reminded of that roll call of dignitaries in Luke's Gospel: "Tiberius Caesar, Pontius Pilate, Herod, Philip, Lysanias, Annas, Caiaphas...." And what comes next? "the word of God came unto John"(Luke 3:1, 2)! All these VIPs only provided background for one prophet in the wilderness! In the balances of God, David Livingstone outweighs a whole succession of kings and queens. Not many wise, mighty, and noble are called anyway. God's *Who's Who* bears no resemblance to ours. One lone Christian who has lost his life to find it, buried as a grain of wheat in a dark pagan land, outshines all the big names of this poor world. David Livingstone knew the great secret. He outlived himself, for he was a great example of planted—not packaged—Christianity.

It might be a disturbing thought to most of our smug church folks that every Christian is meant to be a missionary. We cannot pass the buck of personal responsibility to a few who are engaged in "full-time Christian service." We live in the midst of paganism right here in America. If we are not called to cross the sea, we can cross the street and seek to convert the heathen. Idol worship in Africa is no worse than idle worship in America. Even the church needs missionaries, for it has been said that the greatest evangelistic field is the membership of the average church. A David Livingstone today does not cope with the same types of problems, but the fundamentals are unchanged.

David Livingstone's heart was buried in Africa. Where the heart is, there is the treasure also. Where would your heart be buried if the same procedure were followed with you as with the great missionary? It would be a revealing thing if in all cemeteries it could be written: HERE LIES THE BODY OF _____, BUT HIS HEART IS BURIED _____ *where?*

It could be said in Africa: HERE LIES THE HEART OF DAVID LIVINGSTONE. Where would such a marker be set up for your heart? In some place of business, some unholy affection, some pursuit of prosperity or pleasure? Sometimes a man's hobby is his god, and after he dies his heart might properly be interred in his boat; or some poor soul might order that hers be cremated and put in a box on the bridge table. No wonder we read here and there in the Scriptures: BUT THEIR HEART _____. Ah, there's the rub.

Where lies *your* heart now? Would it be embarrassing if it were buried where it belongs?

CHAPTER 37

Angel Ahead

ALL my life I have been a stickler for getting there on time. In the days of train travel, I was always at the hometown Greensboro station before the train left Danville, Virginia, fifty miles away.

I grew up before traffic lights came along. I have often thought that if I had started reading while waiting for red to turn green, I could have been through the *Encyclopaedia Britannica* by now.

One of my weaknesses has been anticipating trouble that never came. As I look back over the years, I do not recall missing many, if any, important connections; but in my imagination I have failed to make it several hundred times.

As I write this, I am crossing the Atlantic on a BOAC-747. I have a close schedule if I catch my flight home from New York. As usual, I have conjured up visions of a hang-up going through customs, slow traffic on the way from Kennedy to LaGuardia. There is no end to what a fertile imagination can dream up. It is always wise to expect the best—but be prepared for the worst. I seem to have a knack of expecting the worst while I pray for the best!

There is some kinship between all of us and the women on their way to our Lord's sepulcher wondering who would roll away the stone. When they got there they found that an angel had taken care of it. How many times I have worried about the "stone at the sepulcher" and stayed awake at night planning its removal. Somehow I didn't count much on the heavenly helper, and how convicted I have been when my lack of faith was reproved! The angel had been there ahead of me!

Many dear souls have wondered about their acceptance in heaven when they reach the hour of death. It was an old saint who said, "Forefancy your deathbed." It is good counsel, but not a few Christians do it with considerable trepidation. One of the most familiar is Mr. Fearing in *Pilgrim's Progress*. Although a true believer, he was tormented all his days by the haunting fear that he might not reach heaven at last. A timid soul, he never dared claim with certainty many joys he might have known. As Maclaren put it, he managed to distil a bitter vinegar of self-accusation out of grand words in the Bible that were meant to afford the wine of gladness and of consolation. He trembled when he should have triumphed, sighed when he should have sung. But he had the root of the matter in him; and Bunyan tells us that when Mr. Fearing finally reached the river, it was at its lowest, and he got across "not much above wet-shod."

One may think he is going to heaven when he is not, and another may think he is not going when he is. False diffidence is better than false confidence. Now we should not be fearful and doubtful, and this is no justification for Mr. Fearing. He should have gone through this world in a better mood. But some of us are so constructed that Satan plays a lot of melancholy tunes on our heartstrings. Mr. Fearing is not a good specimen of victorious Christianity. But a bruised reed God will not break, and smoking flax He will not quench (see Isaiah 42:3). He knows our frame and remembers that we are dust. If we have put our feeble faith in him it will avail more than mighty faith in anything else. And when we get to the river, he will see to it that the water is low and we shall get over "not much above wet-shod."

P.S. We made that plane connection! The angel got there first.

CHAPTER 38

Testimony of a "Cured" Tourist

I was almost forty when I got married, sixty-six before I bought an automobile, and nearly seventy before I took a trip abroad. (I wanted to think it over!) On the trip I went with old friends whose company was a delight, saw much, and felt more of the charm and challenge of historic places. For all of that I am grateful and shall preserve the blessings received in book or sermon.

But for foreign travel as such I have no good word. I waited a long time to go and used to think I was cheating myself. Now I am grateful that I spared myself the misery for so long. For crowded airports, customs hang-ups, doubtful food, not enough water, crazy eating and sleeping hours, baggage headaches, trying to keep up with passports and health cards, money-changing worse than the Lord cleared out of the temple, how much to take, how little to take, how many headache pills, stomach pills, sleeping pills (I don't use them), air-sickness pills, time-zone exhaustion—I've had it, and you can have it from now on. The most welcome sight is the Statue of Liberty. Mr. Nixon was right: "The best way to appreciate America is to take a trip somewhere else."

Foreign travel just isn't my cup of tea. Hereafter when I need a vacation I think we'll go in the Buick up to the mountains and put up in a quiet little lodge on the Blue Ridge Parkway. Better than anything Europe has to offer would be a few days back in Jugtown where I grew up and a stroll out the old road to watch the sun go down and listen to the wood thrush sing his vespers at the end of a perfect day.

By the time you have sat all day cramped in an airplane, you long for the old days of train travel. Some of us will never understand by what imbecility we deserted the Pullmans with room to walk around and a chance to see the country instead of a sea of clouds.

I suppose I wasn't made for progress—and I don't feel embarrassed. It is no disgrace to feel more at home in simpler places living at slower paces.

Getting in and out of customs, being checked and X-rayed, is another necessary evil. I never did enjoy being examined, even by a doctor. And being frisked makes me feel like a shoplifter who has just been caught in a department store. I'm not fond of the European custom of serving coffee or tea after the meal. I've always wanted my drink along with my vittles. But the Europeans do it that way; and no matter how you may implore, they blissfully do it their way according to a fixed law of the Medes and Persians. Tea after dessert just isn't my cup of tea!

Well, I don't have to do it again. I'm not about to catch the bug of tourism. The only place I'm "getting up a load" for is heaven. I don't think there will be any complaints from the party when that journey ends. I hope heaven won't be as hard to get into!

Of course, I never could have gained the blessings I did reap if I had not put up with the inconveniences of the journey. So in the Christian life the bitter goes with the sweet. I mean to continue the Christian life; but as a foreign tourist, I'm "cured."

CHAPTER 39

Time Out for a Hermit Thrush

ARTHUR Krock relates a charming story about Theodore Roosevelt. He says that the colonel was receiving a line of guests when he suddenly stopped the procession to take one man aside for an animated chat. Everybody wondered what could be of such prime importance; and after it was over someone asked, "What was the president discussing with you?" The reply was something like this: "I'm an amateur ornithologist, and the president saw a bird at his home yesterday which he thought was a hermit thrush. He was checking with me for additional confirmation just to make sure."

My esteem for Theodore Roosevelt went up several more points after I read that. Any man who can stop a line of dignitaries and forget affairs of state long enough to talk about a hermit thrush is a rare specimen in any day or generation. Their breed is scarce.

Teddy Roosevelt did not let the presidency kill him as some have done. While it has wrecked the health of other White House occupants, the colonel thrived on it. Instead of being exhausted, he came out feeling like a "bull moose," to use his own expression, and took off for Africa to hunt lions! The secret lay in his many interests and varied enthusiasms. Not the least of these was his love for the outdoors and nature study. A state dinner was for him no greater thrill than identifying a new warbler. He lived life to the hilt and drank from many fountains.

It would be a fine thing if some pompous notables of today could take time out for a hermit thrush. We are so swollen with a sense of our importance that it would be beneath our dignity to halt the procession for a chat about something simple and old-fashioned. In this synthetic and superficial age we have cut the ties that linked us with basic and elemental values. A few precious things have not changed. The birds still sing the songs birds used to sing, and nothing refreshes the soul like escaping from the rat race somebody misnamed progress to hear a thrush at sundown. If we are to keep our sanity, we had better find time and place for that.

Good men in and out of the presidency have killed themselves over issues that probably were not worth it. I know ministers who need to stop the receiving line, as it were, and "take time for a hermit thrush." The devil—with the assistance of some church people—has set up a schedule for the average preacher today that would require a dozen men to carry out. He is expected to be everything but a prophet, and if he is to be a prophet he will need to "stop the procession" and get away to the woods. Most earthbound deacons would never understand that, of course, and the Ladies Missionary Society would erupt in horror. Our Lord set an example for all Christians when he "stopped the procession" (as it were) to get away to the Sea of Galilee or the Mount of Olives. He sometimes left the pressing multitudes with all their needs to retire for meditation and prayer.

He is a wise man who "takes time out for a hermit thrush," who can "stop the procession" and make a place for the basic simplicities without which the procession means nothing anyway.

6/13/2023
4:54AM
Tuesday

Chapter 40

Foretaste of Glory

THIS gorgeous summer afternoon finds me on a high hill in southern Ohio overlooking Seneca Lake peacefully reposing among the mountains that surround it. This has been my best summer for lovely scenes and soul-stirring sights both at home and abroad. It has been a great season; and now as summer wanes and autumn nears, this blessed spot speaks peace in a serene finale to crown these months of travel.

The cicadas remind me that fall is not far away. The birds sing longer in the mountains. Down in the level country they seem to run out of inspiration, and the heat smothers their exuberance. This morning I have heard the wood thrush, indigo bunting, yellowthroat, field and chipping sparrow, pewee, towhee, yellow-breasted chat, robin, red-eyed vireo.

About six o'clock an automobile horn in one of the parked cars went on a rampage and blew a trumpet blast until one of the preachers staying here got to it. I told the brethren in the morning conference hour that maybe the Lord was trying to wake them up for prayer, but I think they went back to sleep. Last summer about this time I preached for some days to Tennessee preachers in another mountain retreat. This time it is Ohio preachers. One of the good things God has allowed me to enjoy all these years is the fellowship of so many of his ministers. In this span of over five decades of preaching I have known only a few preachers who have disgraced their holy calling. Most of them have the root of the matter in them and would not have become preachers to start with if they had not heard somehow a divine call. There is a trend in some quarters to downgrade preachers, but no puny comments from fussy critics can change the status of God's prophets. Their place is assured, and no effort to reduce them to mere helps and equippers of the laity will cancel their special office in God's economy.

One could wish, in such a spot as this, that all the world might have such peace as blesses this tranquil scene. I know that I am looking out on a torn and troubled world sick unto death in the agony of the end time. No cunning tricks of politicians, no clever bargaining with demonism and anarchy will avail. The whole creation groans and travails awaiting the manifestation of the sons of God. Our Lord will bring peace when he returns. But this restful scene whets the appetite for what is to come, for if it can be this lovely in a world wrecked and marred, what will it be like when the glory of the Lord shall cover the earth as the waters cover the sea?

Thank God for these blessed intervals when we escape from the din and tumult. It is an earnest of things to come even as the assurance of salvation is a "foretaste of glory divine." Man has just about devastated the beautiful world God gave him. Now he is in a dither about ecology and pollution in a belated effort to salvage something from the disaster. I am not very excited about the prospects of his success, but I know that the redemption of creation is part of God's plan for the future.

So I rest here and look in hope, not to environment experts in Washington but to a higher authority who has better blueprints and the power to get the job done in his own good time.

Chapter 41

Astronauts and Anarchists

I sat in a city motel and watched on television that engineering feat of first magnitude—astronauts taking off for the moon. I could turn around in my chair and look out my window at a park across the street where I dared not walk for fear of thugs and thieves. In vivid contrast I beheld the wonder of man's ingenuity on one hand and the moral depravity of man on the other. While three men race toward the stars, other men creep in the slime. Astronauts and anarchists! While some travel to the moon I cannot walk in the park!

Progress is a farce because man's head and hand have created wonders that stun the imagination, but his heart does not keep step; and his morals undo all that his mind has wrought. It would seem that we might wake up sometime and learn a thing or two. I know the adage that all we learn from history is that we learn nothing from history, but at least it ought to cure us of our pride. Civilizations come and go, and usually they run a cycle from rags to riches to rot. This is the most advanced civilization in terms of scientific achievement—now that we have split the atom, gone to the moon, and discovered DNA. But there has been no advance in the things of the spirit, and it has been said that science without conscience is the ruin of the soul.

I was also impressed that day in my motel room by the irony of spending millions to go to the moon when so much cries for instant help here on earth. The experts have gotten us into the worst mess of all time, and every area of modern life is a shambles of confusion. Man has not only learned how to blow the race into oblivion, he has poisoned the air, and contaminated the water until he threatens to exterminate himself with the wastes of his own inventions. We grumble at having to boil drinking water abroad, but at home we load it with chemicals until I haven't had a good drink of it lately.

Exploring space nowadays is a kind of escapism. If we could humbly acknowledge our failure and turn to God, we could find wisdom enough to handle our science and make it our servant instead of our master. The world of science is not under the rule of Jesus Christ, although some scientists are Christians. The world by and large is run by the once-born, not by the twice-born; and the Scriptures hold no promise that the structure and culture of our age will ever bow to the Lordship of the Savior. The Christian is an exile and an alien making his way through a world dominated by the devil. Of course Satan's reign will end and our Lord will take over when he returns, but until then we shall have to put up with such contradictions as I saw from my motel room. This does not mean that we should not clean up the park so that decent people can walk in it; but crime, poverty, and all our other maladies will not be removed by education and legislation. We should make the earth as livable as possible, but the astronauts and anarchists will co-exist until the end when he whose right it is to reign shall return.

So I make my way between scientific advance on one hand and moral decay on the other. I am not unduly exhilirated by the one or overdepressed by the other. On one hand, the machine will never liberate our souls; and on the other, the devil can go only as far as God allows him. Science reigns at one of these poles and sin at the other. Science can never master sin, and sin spoils the blessings of science.

When the Lord sets up his kingdom I will be able to walk in the park with none to molest or make afraid. And in the new age, I will need no astronaut to pilot me to the stars!

CHAPTER 42

"Backlog" Christians

I have been spending this week in Florida in a lovely room with a fireplace. There are other kinds of heating available, but I like to get up of a morning and start a fire. In this push-button age one does not get that opportunity every day. Then, too, it takes me back to boyhood days when I rose early at father's command to build a fire in the old fireplace back home in the country. I was the woodchopper and the wood bringer-inner, and I learned early that making a fire on a winter morning was not such a chilly chore if I got ready the evening before. There must be a big backlog of slow-burning wood, a stout forelog (smaller but substantial), plenty of middle-sized wood and—most important for a quick fire—lots of rich kindling. Newspapers and magazines might help but were unnecessary if the kindling was right. And of course a bed of hot coals from the night before was always a welcome accessory.

Building revival fires in our churches calls for several kinds of Christians, just as the fire in the fireplace calls for several kinds of wood. Sometimes I have spoken or written of the backlog as representing unconverted or undedicated church members, but now I am thinking in terms of temperament and makeup. The church needs kindling-wood Christians, young and old, of the more excitable and fervent type to begin the revival. They are quick to burst into flame and burn up soon, but they serve a good purpose. They spark the conflagration. They detonate the charge. They light the fuse. They are highly inflammable (both for good or evil), they catch the vision quickly, respond readily to the challenge, and are eager to start something.

95

We need also the middle-sized wood—those who are slower to burst into a blaze but who burn longer, being made of more durable material. They are the church members who may not shine dazzlingly but shine daily. They do the drudgery, the day-in-and-day-out work of the church; they keep it going when there is no revival—when the kindling wood has been consumed—when no glowing excitements make headlines. They pay the bills and may be short on romance but are long on reality.

But I must save my best word for the backlogs—those heavier, sturdier types of solid wood. There is no beauty about them—they are oak and not pine. Being short on resin, they do not blaze at the first strike of the match. Indeed the fire may burn a long time before they catch on. But they burn long after the initial flame has died, and one sits late at night before a smouldering backlog that throws out its warmth long after the dancing flames have gone.

I have known backlog Christians and learned long since to value their worth. They may be slow to catch fire during a revival. They may even look with disdain on the blazing kindling-wood members as an old oak might turn a cold shoulder at first to pine splinters. But when they do warm up they wax hot and stay hot and outlast all the more excitable saints and even the middle-sized wood among the church workers. And never forget that the backlog throws out the heat of *all* the wood, for if there were no backlog the rest of the wood would only keep itself warm and furnish little comfort to anybody.

So, dull and prosaic as backlogs may be, I am inclined to give to them highest honor; for they even hold some fire when new kindling wood has to be found.

There is no substitute for "backlog" Christians!

CHAPTER 43

Pilo

DURING a week of meetings in southern Texas I came to know a new member of the church, a young Mexican named Pilo. He was a radiant Christian with all the refreshing exuberance of a simple believer who has not yet met too many Bible scholars. I can only pray that he will not lose that glow as he observes most professing Christians, or have his faith dulled by preaching that doubts or denies the Word of God.

One night Pilo brought a friend to the meetings, another young Mexican who came forward professing faith in Christ. Later we heard that this friend explained his initial interest in Chrstianity by saying, "I wanted to be like Pilo." Pilo had something he did not have but wanted, and he found it in Christ.

Ah, here is the crying shame and desperate need in the church today. There are not enough Pilos whose testimony stirs a hunger in needy hearts to have the same joy in their own. How many Christians do you know who make you want to be like them? Most of our church people are as confused and harassed and defeated as everybody else. Where is the zest, the victory, the inner peace, and outward calm that should be the trademark of God's people?

The churches spend millions trying to "sell" Christianity. Now advertising and promotion have their place, but the best selling agent is somebody who is a living example of the worth of the product. A bald-headed man will have scant success selling hair tonic. We use plenty of raw material but turn out a poor example of all the claims we make. *Christian* is both a noun and an adjective. We are not producing many Christian Christians! It is the poor grade of Christians in our churches that nullifies most of our herculean endeavors to put the gospel across from the pulpit. There are not enough Pilos in the membership. Pilo's friend would probably never have been won by mere church promotion. A visit from a church worker would have made a poor impression. He knew Pilo before and after conversion, and he knew something had happened. If we had enough transformed new creatures in our fellowships we would soon double the membership. Pilo was not a church promoter graduated from some training school with a briefcase full of graphs and charts. He was just a normal Christian living a normal Christian life.

Our Lord did not tell his disciples merely to *bear* witness but to *be* witnesses. One can talk it but not "walk" it. Many a man has been won to Christ by a godly wife when sermons went over his head unheeded. Somebody you want to be like is an influence for good or evil more powerful than any other.

It is high time that we specialized in our churches in the school of Christ, producing advanced postgraduates in Christian maturity. We are embarrassed by dropouts and delinquents whose homework and report cards are a disgrace. We have gone in for quantity, but our quality is a shame to the cause we champion.

We do not need more promoters—we need more Pilos!

Chapter 44

Hop-O-My-Thumb

I walked along a drab city street on a lonely winter day. Birds were so few and spring so far away that my harp was hung on the willows and my spirits in sore need of cheer. Suddenly my ear picked up the faintest sound in a nearby tree, and my eyes caught a fleeting glimpse. A tiny ruby-crowned kinglet and his mite of a mate chanced by. They were gone in an instant, but they changed the morning for me. It was a visit from another realm. The smallest delegation imaginable had called on me from the bird kingdom so scantily represented in these chilly months so far from spring. We gladly take what we can get these days, and a kinglet is something extra special. Although he is a winter bird he is never so plentiful that we take him for granted.

John Burroughs called kinglets "Hop-O-My-Thumbs." They are the smallest of our feathered tribe except for the humming-bird. This little fellow was about the size of the first part of my thumb, but his energy was all out of proportion to his size. Moreover, his warble is so loud for a larynx the size of a pinhead that someone has said: "If the strength of the human voice were in the same proportion to the size of the larynx, we could converse at ease at a distance of a mile or more."

What amazes me most is the astounding hardihood of this tiny elf. He thrives on the bitterest of cold weather. When other birds give up the fight, and the freezing blasts would drive the most rugged logswoodsman to shelter, the kinglet is having the time of his life. When it is too rough for everybody else it is just getting right for him. I shall never understand what kind of batteries the good Lord packed into this mini-bird's frame, or how such a torrent of energy can be compressed into this thimble of a creature. Then too, he is just as cheerful as his larger cousin, the chickadee. They are good friends and take the winter as it comes. I know there are very learned explanations of the disparity between the kinglet's size and his voice, his energy and his hardihood—but I still marvel. It just doesn't add up by ordinary standards. To sing like that he should be the size of a robin, and to endure such weather he should have the constitution of an eagle. It leads me to suspect that the Creator has a scale of his own and confounds us again and again with how much he can pack into the infinitesimal, whether it be atoms or kinglets.

He does wonders along this line with us human beings. Who has not heard of some frail little woman (by all ordinary calculations as fragile as a butterfly), yet bearing burdens and doing the work of a dozen others—supposed to be dead but refusing to die—outliving robust men and putting even the predictions of doctors to shame? God has a scale of his own; and as our day is, he makes our strength to be, to the discomfiture of all the experts. It is the only way to explain the pioneers, the apostle Paul, and some of our dads and mothers of earlier days. It is possible to lay hold of God for body, mind, and spirit all out of proportion to our natural strength. If the endurance of a giant can be set in the tiny frame of a kinglet, shame on us if we measure the Niagara of God's power by the size of our little pitcher! To them that have no might, he increaseth strength; and he can endow us with a force all out of proportion to our frame.

Hop-O-My-Thumb shames me in my heated apartment by the way he breezes through the blizzards. The lives of God's great souls ought to make red the faces of us protected saints in these days of cushioned living. Look not at your frail equipment. The Almighty is able to supercharge you with sufficient grace to endure hardness as his good soldier and sing your way through the worst storms the devil can invent.

Never mind the disproportions. His strength is made perfect in weakness.

CHAPTER 45

"Pause for Station Identification...."

TO all television viewers it is a familiar announcement. In the middle of the program comes a halt, and we are informed of the source from which it comes. We live today in a bewildering bedlam, our eardrums battered by a thousand voices, some from God and some from the devil, some from heaven and some from hell. If we are to keep our sanity we must take time for station identification. Some Christians are so confused that they cannot distinguish the voice of the Holy Spirit from the voice of Satan. We must try the spirits whether they be of God, because many false Christs and false prophets are gone out into the world. Our Lord warned us about both and told us that they would deceive many. Satan is disguised as an angel of light.

No gift of God is scarcer and at the same time more necessary than the discerning of spirits. The natural man knows nothing about it. The carnal man is devoid of it. Only the spiritual man may have it.

How to identify your station? Ask God for wisdom (*see* James 1:5). Ask in faith, nothing wavering, for the wavering man is like the storm-tossed billow of the sea. Use the guidelines for discerning truth and error (*see* John 4:2, 3). And remember that you have the Word of God, the greatest discerner of all (*see* Hebrews 4:12), living, powerful, and sharper than a two-edged sword. Any man with that much discernment available at any time has no business saying he cannot identify his station!

Best of all, let him keep close to the Good Shepherd. His sheep hear his voice, he knows them and they follow him. They know his voice and they know not the voice of strangers. The man who knows real money well can easily spot the counterfeit.

But station identification calls for a pause. Men are deceived and listen to wrong stations because they are never still long enough to check the log. They tune in on wavelengths from the wrong station. Some of it may be very exciting, the music catchy, and the voice alluring. Things are said that sound heavenly though they originated in hell. Satan can be angelic, quote Scripture, and sing hymns. He is the master imitator and can simulate the work of God even as Jannes and Jambres performed like Moses.

Modern living is geared to a tempo that leaves no time for pauses. So we have a befuddled generation in a wild stampede mistaking Satan for God and hell for heaven. Unless we resolutely make time for station identification we shall go down with them.

Even the pauses work in a little commercial or two. It is typical of the times. It may not be possible for this generation to get still except by the aid of tranquilizers. We may be too far gone. It is a major operation these days to achieve solitude. It is significant that we are in the midst of a charismatic upheaval along with absolute silence about discerning of spirits. It is high time we paused for station identification to get our bearings on all the issues. It is a sad commentary on the age that radio and television must be left on all day and most of the night. We are afraid of the silence—lest we think. It is time to check the station. The devil is the prince of the power of the air and his network never signs off. He jams the voice of heaven by a thousand devices.

Blessed is he who still knows how to tune in on God!

CHAPTER 46

A Day in Disney World

SARA and I visited Disney World and were swallowed up in sixty thousand tourists from everywhere. I soon found myself calling it Dizzy World! Why does this avalanche of people descend on this land of fantasy? For one reason—because it is an escape from reality. Everybody is trying to get away from it all. Some go to the movies or opera, some to the ball game. Some play bridge all afternoon. When we were children we read *Alice in Wonderland, Cinderella, Robinson Crusoe, The Wizard of Oz.* Some take the wrong road and turn to drugs, alcohol, immorality, religious orgies, demonic cults, magic. Walt Disney was a genius who created a wonderland of innocent make-believe enjoyed by adults and children alike. Don't forget that Dad spends more time than Junior playing with the electric train he bought for his son!

But one does not have to go to Disney World or to any Shangri-La to get away from it all. We do not have to escape from reality. There are two worlds of Reality—the natural and the spiritual.... "the things which are seen are temporal; but the things which are not seen are eternal" (2 Corinthians 4:18). We can live in another world while we live in this one—in a world of spiritual reality in the midst of this present natural world. Jesus came to tell us about the kingdom of heaven. All who trust and follow him belong to that kingdom. Christians are not citizens of earth trying to get to heaven but citizens of heaven making their way through this world.

The keys to this kingdom are conversion and childlikeness (see Matthew 18:3). When we are born again, we enter a second childhood as children of God. Some are worldly, some are unworldly, some are otherworldly. A little boy in a parade of youngsters was marching out of step. It turned out that he had a transistor radio under his coat and was keeping step with music from a thousand miles away! So does the Christian march through this world keeping step with the drumbeats of heaven. He does not stand on Jordan's stormy banks casting a wishful eye toward Canaan—he dwells now in Beulah Land. He tastes the powers of the age to come. The blessed assurance that Jesus is his is a foretaste of glory divine.

This other world is not a make-believe realm of fantasy. We *know* that we are dead and risen with Christ. We accept it, affirm it, and act upon it. The childlike Christian has a sense of wonder far more marvelous than the delight of a youngster in Disney World. He is a new creature to whom all things have become new. He drinks of a new wine that leaves no hangover. There will be trouble and hardship as we pilgrims and strangers, exiles and aliens travel toward that city with foundations whose builder and maker is God. We groan in this tabernacle; but we know that all things work together for good to us, and that our light affliction (which is but for a moment) works for us a far more exceeding and eternal weight of glory.

The early church shook that age because it had learned to live in two worlds at once with a simple faith, a pilgrim character, and a blessed hope. Then Constantine came along and made Christianity popular and the church at home in this world. We need a new band of pilgrims who make their way through these lowlands in childlike wonder while creation stands on tiptoe waiting for the manifestation of the sons of God—those who "ply their daily task with busier feet because their secret souls a holier strain repeat."

They do not escape from reality—they triumph over it and find a life more wonderful than all the Disney Worlds that man could ever devise.

CHAPTER 47

Mr. Fixit

I don't know what they'd do at the church if it weren't for Mr. Fixit. Call him janitor, custodian, sexton, handyman, caretaker—what you will—he is the odd-job specialist. He keeps all the machinery moving. He has no degree from any school ("Just picked it up," he says), but he can repair the typewriter, mend the furniture, tend the furnace, clean up the rooms, adjust the air conditioning, keep the lights burning, locate lost articles, mow the grass. On occasion he tunes up the pastor's balky automobile, clears up the television picture, oils squeaky doors, helps in the kitchen. Much of what he does is really not in his department, but Mr. Fixit doesn't draw the line between what he gets paid for doing and what he doesn't. Indeed it is not easy to define just what his "department" is! He loves the Lord and loves the church and his is a labor of love. And love isn't too finicky about drawing lines as to the boundaries of its province.

The pastor is a Th.D. and the staff are highly trained helpers, and the things they do are quite impressive—but the whole business would grind to a halt without Mr. Fixit behind the scenes. Nobody seems to be aware that he is around, but they would soon be aware if he were not around! All the suppers and dramas and concerts and cantatas and the big Sunday services would be a comedy of errors without the flitting figure here and there between blown-out fuses and broken-down loudspeakers, cold coffee and not enough doughnuts, and all the snafus that plague the good Lord's work.

Multiply Mr. Fixit several thousand times and you have a tribe of unsung heroes who spend their days just keeping the stages set for the prima donnas who get all the glory. What

105

would the VIPs do without the obscure unknowns who do the dirty work? There are some notables in the Lord's work that we could get along without. Somehow the church would roll on if they left us—it always has. But I shudder to think what would happen if all the Mr. Fixits went on strike!

These are they of olden times who got up early and trudged to little country churches to make fires in the wood-burning stove. These are they who sit in the nursery and miss the sermon listening to a roomful of bawling babies. They couldn't sing a solo or teach a class, and to speak in public would frighten them out of their wits. But theirs will be the reward for a multitude of little duties faithfully done. They are not seen in the pictures of big events, but if it were not for them half of the big events wouldn't happen.

I propose a Mr. Fixit Day when we pause to honor what the New Testament calls "helps" (see 1 Corinthians 12:28). If we never do it there will be such a day at the Great Assize when the Master passes out the rewards. On that day some VIPs will shrivel up and some nonentities will come into their own. Theirs will be the citation as in Matthew 25:21: "Thou hast been faithful over a few things."

"As is his part that goeth down to the battle, so shall his part be that tarrieth by the stuff! they shall part alike" (1 Samuel 30:24). I have a feeling that the unknown Christian who trimmed the old kerosene lamps a hundred years ago or fixed the amplifier yesterday will get a magna cum laude along with some famous preacher.

Apostles, prophets, and teachers would fare poorly without "helps." Their labor is too often taken for granted—but God knows them. They seek no laurels and wear no halos. They want no trumpet sounded before them. They had rather be doorkeepers in the house of the Lord than dwell in the tents of wickedness (see Psalms 84:10).

I do not think repairs will be necessary in heaven; but if they were, there will be plenty of Mr. Fixits there who have served a good apprenticeship down here.

CHAPTER 48

Pre-Aldersgate Wesley

SOME time ago I visited the Methodist campground, Epworth-by-the-sea on the Georgia coast. In this historic area John Wesley labored over two centuries ago. Imagine a chapel that had as ministers John and Charles Wesley and George Whitefield! On these grounds there is a marker placed there by Bishop Arthur Moore bearing this inscription:

> LET US READ THE STORY OF JOHN WESLEY AGAIN. THIS CULTURED, CONSCIENTIOUS GENTLEMAN, RESOLUTE IN SELF-DENIAL, PUNCTUAL IN ALL OBSERVANCES, DOING ALL THE GOOD HE COULD, AND AVOIDING EVIL, HAD EVERYTHING BUT PEACE IN HIS OWN HEART. THEN THE ROOM IN ALDERSGATE STREET AND HIS FACE-TO-FACE CONFRONTATION WITH HIS SAVIOUR. PRESENTLY THAT MASTERFUL LITTLE MAN CLIMBED ON HIS HORSE TO SET OUT ON THE CONQUEST OF ENGLAND, WITH ONLY ONE RESOURCE, THE ASSURANCE GIVEN HIM THAT CHRIST HAD TAKEN AWAY HIS SINS. SOON THAT SPARK OF GRACE SET TEN THOUSAND HEARTS ON FIRE.

As I strolled and meditated on that sacred spot, I remembered that John Wesley's mother was one of earth's godliest women, that his father, both grandfathers and great-grandfather were all ministers; that he himself was an Oxford man, deeply religious and a missionary who came all the way to America to convert others—but asking all the time, "Who will convert me?" Never did a man have more qualifications for the ministry without being ready to preach. It was not until he returned to

England and that little meeting on Aldersgate Street that he was ignited by a spark from heaven, and flamed into one of the most amazing human firebrands of all time.

I am smitten with the uneasy feeling that the professing church today—in all its herculean labors with so little to show for it—is like the pre-Aldersgate Wesley. Remember that John Wesley was a mighty worker before his own heart was strangely warmed. No one questions the earnestness, the sincerity, the stupendous toil of the present-day church; but there is lacking the spark that detonates the charge. Facts and formulas and finances are in evidence, but where is the fire? There is strange fire and, alas, stage fire; but where is the flame that set England ablaze over two centuries ago?

So much of what we are doing today is pre-Pentecost. The disciples had known our Lord, had walked with him, had heard him preach, and seen him heal; they had performed wonders themselves, but they were not ready to face the world of their time until there came the rushing wind and the tongues of fire. One thinks of Isaiah, a patrician prophet and a spiritual nobleman, but not ready to say, "Here am I" until first he had said, "Woe is me!" and his tongue had felt the coal from off the altar.

Whatever we call it theologically, the event that sets a man apart for God must be a divine confrontation. It may be as tempestuous as a hurricane—or as quiet as an autumn sunset—but something must happen that cannot be supplied by education or personality or ability or the best of intentions. Pentecost indeed happened once for all as an event in history, but the experience of it can be repeated in every age as often as a Wesley meets his Aldersgate.

Here is the answer to our feverish and futile striving in the church today. There is too much pre-Aldersgate Wesley about it all. What he needed was not the challenge he saw in America so much as the change he felt at Aldersgate. He admitted his need and God met him.

Could we but bring ourselves to a like admission, God would meet us. But we are rich and increased with goods and have need of nothing, and so a revolution like that which started with John Wesley—and shook a nation—is waiting today to begin.

CHAPTER 49

The Unhurried Dawn

JOB lamented: "When I lie down, I say, When shall I arise and the night be gone? and I am full of tossings to and fro until the dawning of the day" (7:4). The psalmist declared: "My soul waiteth for the Lord more than they that watch for the morning: I say, more than they that watch for the morning"(Psalms 130:6).

I am now in the age category of those who rise up at the voice of the bird (see Ecclesiastes 12:4). Many mornings I await the dawn of the new day and have wished at times that I could press a button and turn it on as I do my heat or light. But sunrise has not yet been mastered by our gadgets (thank the Lord), and in my better moments I rejoice that in this age of maddening speed there are still a few things that cannot be hurried.

It is a blessed thing that man cannot get his impatient hands on the machinery of the Almighty. We have not done too well lately with what secrets we have mastered. I write these lines in the Ozarks where I am awakened each morning by the robin outside, and I lie for awhile watching darkness turn to day. There is no way to hurry it. Within a few days we will change our watches to daylight savings time, one of the many funny things we are doing these days. It will not have the slightest effect on the sun coming up. It is springtime now, but springtime cannot be speeded. God takes his time with the seasons.

Today we want to tear open the cocoon and get the butterfly out too soon. At breakfast I find instant coffee, instant cereal—everything is instant. We must have it now—we cannot wait. But other things besides coffee need to percolate. We have tried to hurry up childhood, and we make our youngsters into adults

111

before they are well in their teens. The result is a crop of preco-cious kids—all vine and no roots.

We try to rush the processes of God in spiritual matters. The Word of God is not a bomb set to explode all of a sudden. It is seed, and seed requires time to sprout. We must see immediate results. A man can be converted in a moment, but even then as a rule many forces have been at work long before the climax. In the making of a Christian it takes time to be holy as the old song exhorts us. Think how patient our Lord was with Simon Peter. Simon was not made into a rock overnight.

A popular song was titled, *The World Is Waiting for the Sunrise.* Indeed it is, but we are trying to hurry the dawn of that day by revolution. Wild reformers would burn down the establishment, but they have nothing to put in its place. That blessed new day will not be ushered in by education, legislation, reformation. It will come when our Lord returns, and he that shall come will come and will not tarry. We are impatient; but although God may seem slow, he is never late.

"Be patient therefore, brethren, until the coming of the Lord. Behold, the husbandman waiteth for the precious fruit of the earth, and hath long patience for it, until he receive the early and latter rain. Be ye also patient; stablish your hearts: for the coming of the Lord draweth nigh" (James 5:7, 8).

Throughout the Bible the word is *Wait.* The world wants a push-button millennium, but the Christian awaits the unhurried dawn.

CHAPTER 50

Home from School

THIS morning I slipped back sixty years into the past and strolled along the paths of my boyhood. I returned to Jugtown, and what is left of old scenes that fond recollection has enshrined in the temple of memory. I made my way through woods once familiar and across the little stream where often I lingered in gentler and simpler days. It was about the time I had my first automobile ride, holding on for dear life while we must have made thirty miles an hour. Last week I crossed the Atlantic in six hours on a 747. A lot of water has run down that creek I crossed this morning since I looked for crawfishes in it in the early years of this century!

I tried to find the place where Hog Hill School used to stand. I had no success, but on my jaunt I made a precious discovery. New hard-surface roads are everywhere, but I found several hundred yards of the old dirt road—the same old road I walked as a boy to and from that little one-teacher school. It came back to me like yesterday, that little band of country kids who didn't have much and didn't know much and didn't want much. I remembered the old slate for writing, and the few books, and my tin dinner box with the sweet potato and hunk of fatback. I had good health and a good home and good friends. We were not spoiled brats who had tried everything. There were things wrong with the establishment, but we weren't out to burn it down. Life was wholesome and plain, and we were just ordinary country young'uns with not a wild and woolly freak in the crowd.

We trudged that old road fresh and happy of a morning. I enjoyed the hour at noon when we could play. By afternoon we were a bit worn from arithmetic and geography and spelling and

113

playing ante-over and what passed for baseball. So we sort of loafed along at a languid pace home from school.

The decades have passed, and that old gang of mine has few survivors. I stood quietly on that old road this morning and reflected. I'm past threescore and ten, but I'm still in school. It is the school the Savior meant when he said, "Take my yoke upon you and learn of me" (Matthew 11:29). I've been a student a long, long time. I'm afraid I've been a poor learner, and I don't think I'll make magna cum laude. My homework has often failed, and my report card has not shown many As. But I'm not a dropout, and I'd like to finish at the Great Commencement Day with the Master's "Well done." I must be getting pretty close to graduation, and I'd like to finish my course and, as Sam Jones put it, "Go home to God as happy as any schoolboy ever went home from school."

So I walked that old, old road this morning, deeply conscious that I'm still coming home from school. With sixty years to study I should have made better grades. I ought to be in graduate school, whereas I am still barely out of kindergarten. But there is an eternity ahead, and the contrast between now and then will be greater than the difference between this little schoolhouse of my boyhood and the greatest university.

And I am upheld by that sweetly solemn thought that comes to me o'er and o'er—that I am nearer home than I've ever been before.

6/14/2023
8:53AM
CDES

Bravo Vance!
And
Thank you

To obtain additional copies of this book, and to see a list of
other great Christian titles, including more by
Vance Havner, visit our web site:
www.KingsleyPress.com

Made in United States
North Haven, CT
20 May 2023

36792085R00065